AESTHETICS ACROSS THE COLOR LINE

AESTHETICS ACROSS THE COLOR LINE

Why Nietzsche (Sometimes) Can't Sing the Blues

James J. Winchester

ROWMAN & LITTLEFIELD PUBLISHERS, INC.
Lanham • Boulder • New York • Oxford

ROWMAN & LITTLEFIELD PUBLISHERS, INC.

Published in the United States of America
by Rowman & Littlefield Publishers, Inc.
A Member of the Rowman & Littlefield Publishing Group
4720 Boston Way, Lanham, Maryland 20706
www.rowmanlittlefield.com

12 Hid's Copse Road
Cumnor Hill, Oxford OX2 9JJ, England

Copyright © 2002 by Rowman & Littlefield Publishers, Inc.

All rights reserved. No part of this publication may be reproduced, stored in a retrieval system, or transmitted in any form or by any means, electronic, mechanical, photocopying, recording, or otherwise, without the prior permission of the publisher.

British Library Cataloguing in Publication Information Available

Library of Congress Cataloging-in-Publication Data

Winchester, James J.
 Aesthetics across the color line : why Nietzsche (sometimes) can't sing the blues / James J. Winchester.
 p. cm.
 Includes bibliographical references and index.
 ISBN 0-7425-1390-4 (alk. paper) - ISBN 0-7425-1391-2 (pbk. : alk. paper)
 1. Nietzsche, Friedrich Wilhelm, 1844–1900—Aesthetics. I. Title.
 B3318.A4 W56 2002
 111'.85- dc21   2002006869

Printed in the United States of America

∞ ™ The paper used in this publication meets the minimum requirements of American National Standard for Information Sciences—Permanence of Paper for Printed Library Materials, ANSI/NISO Z39.48-1992.

To Sophie and Adrian

CONTENTS

Acknowledgments	ix
Introduction: Understanding the Art of Others	1
1 Understanding Aesthetic Judgments across Cultural Borders	17
2 Why Nietzsche (Sometimes) Can't Sing the Blues; or, Davis, Nietzsche, and the Social Embeddedness of Aesthetic Judgments	45
3 Misunderstanding Aesthetic Judgments across Cultural Divides	73
4 Adorno, Jazz, and the Limits of Apprenticeship	99
5 Art and the Politics of Representation in the South Bronx	121
Index	141
About the Author	145

ACKNOWLEDGMENTS

My daughter has instructed me that since my first book was dedicated to my wife and several of my dearest friends, this book should be dedicated to her brother and herself. Of course she is right. Having made a joint decision to bring the two of them into the world, there have been many times over the last six years when I have entrusted them to the care of others so that I might write this book. With Sophie and Adrian I share a love of books and art, and it is with great love that I dedicate this book to them. My wife Eve was already included in the dedication of my first book, but nonetheless she clearly has earned my continued thanks not only for the way that she has encouraged and supported the writing of this book but also for the role she has played in opening up several of the worlds of Africa to me as well as teaching me much about communication between men and women.

A book about understanding across cultural divides would never have been possible if many had not undertaken the sometimes arduous but often exhilarating task of trying to understand me and my world and opening up their worlds to me. I thank my parents and my brother and sister, who were always very open to learning about other cultures and taught me from a very young age to welcome people from other cultures as well as providing me with a love of learning. During my academic training I was extremely fortunate to have known a variety of people, professors and fellow students, from all over the world. I have traveled extensively for more than twenty-five years and cannot begin to name all of those whom I have met and who have helped me to gain an understanding of other cultures. The following is a very short list, but to these and many others I owe many thanks for helping to make me more aware of other cultural realms and lovingly embracing me: Bonnie Bortnick,

Joan Dane-Kellogue, Paul Gray, Anne Kohn, Stewart Lerman, Giorgio Tonelli, Françoise and Gene McCreary, Jean Pierre and Mary Lou Blum, Ute Guzzoni, Jean Marie Bonnard, Antoine Ferte, Bogdan Ryzinki, Fabio Morales, German Melendez, Daniella Mateus, Georg Schreiber, Martin Anduschus, Christoph Eyrich, Johanna Schmidt, Charlotte Schmidt, Marco Brusotti, Susan Reichholtz, Annetta Rumele, Michael Theunissen, Wolfgang Mueller-Lauter, Grobli Zirignon, Monique Aggrey, Tanella Boni, Yi Xiyun Zhaobin, Mae LeGrand, Charles Jackson, and Pilkington Ssengendo.

I would like to thank Robert Bernasconi, David Carr, Tim Craker, Christa Davis, Robert Davis, Tod Franklin, Leonard Lawlor, Arturo Lindsay, Rudolf Makkreel, Ronald Moore, Guy Oaks, Louis Ruprecht, Carola Sauter, Jackie Scott, Dennis Schmidt, and Cindy Willett, who have each read portions or all of this book and given me helpful suggestions. They have encouraged me in the writing of this manuscript and helped to make it possible. I would also like to thank the anonymous reviewers who made very helpful suggestions and comments. Eve DeVaro has been a wonderful editor, and I thank her for taking on this project and for all her help in seeing it through.

For ten years I taught at Spelman College, and without that experience I would never have been able to write this book. What follows is only a very partial list of the Spelman students with whom I have worked closely. I learned a great deal from them and will always be thankful for their readiness to enter into dialogue with me. Talking about race in the United States is often difficult, but each of these students has spoken openly and honestly with me about many of the issues I raise in this book: Kristen Agnew, Kia Baldwin, Sylvia Baldwin, Isadora Belle, Taralyn Caudle, Sheri Dennis, Ehimwenma Iyamu, Ayanna Free, Naima Glenn, Jasmine Green, Jennifier Haile, Kafia Haile, Sylvia Hall, Tamra Haywood, Tee Holman, Brandi Iryshe, Cassandra Jackson, Denise James, Kathryn Johnson, Calinda Lee, Tiffany Lovett, Jackie Omotalde, Beth Perry, Raymonda Scrivner, and Anika Simpson. Many of these students are presently pursuing graduate degrees, and two have finished them. I look forward to continued interactions with them in the years ahead as we become colleagues. I have also learned a great deal from and benefited from the encouragement of several of my former Spelman colleagues, including Gena Allah, Peter Chen, Johnetta Cole, Christine Farris, Beverly Guy-Sheftal, Derrick Hylton, Joe Jennings, Stephen Knadler, Harry Lefever, Colm Mulcahy, Opal Moore, Mona Phillips, Cynthia Spence, and Gloria Wade-Gayles.

I have recently taken a new position at Georgia College and State University. I have benefited from conversations with many faculty and students, including Ashleigh Cook, Susan Cummings, Mike Digby, Rosemary DePaolo,

Hank Edmundson, Courtney Ferrell, Daniel Fernald, Chris Grant, Julia Jordan, Mary Magoulick, Katie Moses, John Sallstrum, Debora Vess, and Cliff Wilkerson.

To all of these people and the ones whom I have forgotten as well, I extend my thanks.

Chapter 1 was previously published in the *Southern Journal of Philosophy* 38, no. 3. Parts of chapter 2 were also published in translation in *Nietzsche en perspectiva* (Bogotá, Colombia: Siglo del Hombre, 2001). Parts of chapter 2 will also be published in a forthcoming manuscript from State University of New York Press entitled *Critical Affinities*. I gratefully acknowledge the permission of the journal editors and presses to republish parts of these essays. I have also benefited from the comments that I have received while presenting parts of this book at many different venues. Parts of the introduction were presented to the philosophy department at University of Freiburg in Germany. Sections of chapter 1 were presented at the International Association for Philosophy and Literature. Parts of chapter 2 were presented at the Society for Phenomenology and Existential Philosophy and also at the conference *Nietzsche en Perspective*, in Bogotá, Colombia, and at the Midsouth Philosophy Conference. Parts of chapter 3 were presented at the Georgia Continental Circle and at the International Association for Philosophy and Literature. Parts of chapter 4 were presented to the philosophical seminar at the Technical University Braunschweig in Germany and at the Midsouth Philosophy Conference. For the many helpful comments and suggestions I received I am truly thankful.

INTRODUCTION: UNDERSTANDING THE ART OF OTHERS

> If Bessie Smith was the "world's greatest blues singer," it was at least in part because . . . she brought song and laughter as she evoked the harshest and cruelest experiences of black people in America, and she brought a promise that "the sun's gonna shine in my back door some day."
>
> —Angela Davis, *Blues Legacies and Black Feminism*

Is it possible to understand the art of those who live across cultural borders? I want to know not only whether it is possible to understand what we in the West commonly think of as "art"—that is to say, those pictures that hang in the blockbuster shows of modern museums, and those performances held in venues of high culture; in short I am not interested exclusively in those products of the culture industry traditionally thought of as "art objects"—but also whether we can understand art and the judgments based on feelings about a wide range of creative activities that are made by those living on the other sides of cultural borders.[1]

I believe that cross-cultural understanding of art is possible, but it requires us to study the worlds out of which that art comes. If we want to understand Bessie Smith's music, then we must devote ourselves to learning about not only her art but also the social worlds out of which her life and her art were formed. It is not always easy to understand the worlds of others, but then again, we must constantly cross borders to understand each other, even those closest to us. In what follows, I reflect primarily on problems in aesthetic understanding across racial lines in the United States. Most of my examples are drawn from attempts to understand art and aesthetic judgments across the racial divide between blacks and whites. I often think about my ability as a white male to understand the art and aesthetic judgments of African Americans. W. E. B. Du Bois was prophetic. As he suggested it would be, the twentieth century was

1

the century of the color line in the United States.² This book is an attempt to build bridges across that line even as I recognize that the black–white racial divide is only one of many racial divides in the United States today where bridges need to be built.

The importance of cross-cultural understanding has been brought home to me by my experience of teaching for ten years at Spelman College in Atlanta, Georgia. Spelman is a historically black college for women. I have had the very good fortune to work with many African-American friends, colleagues, and students who were willing to do the sometimes difficult, but often extremely rewarding, work of trying to understand one another across racial and gender divides. In my teaching and scholarship I have employed both "classics" from the history of Western philosophy and works by Angela Davis, Patricia Hill Collins, bell hooks, Cornel West, and Patricia Williams, among others. Some of the lessons learned can be used to help understand the process of communication across other cultural divides, but clearly each constellation of cultural elements poses its own problems as well as its own exciting possibilities. On occasion, this work will reach out to examine the process of understanding the art of non-Western cultures, but I recognize that my work of understanding the art of others is only beginning.

I use the term "culture" in a very wide sense here. Culture, in what follows, refers not only to nations or groups within nations. It also refers to gender, race, class, sexual orientation, and age; in short, any part of our identity that is shaped primarily by human interactions, as opposed to our biology, is cultural. To cite a famous distinction from feminist thought, we are born male or female; in that sense our sex is biological. At the same time, from birth we are taught how to be male or female; therefore our gender is culturally constructed.³ Similarly, we are taught to fulfill particular class, ethnic, race, and many other roles. All human beings play a variety of cultural roles. We must cross borders every day to communicate with even those with whom we are most closely aligned. We must cross generational borders to communicate with our parents. We must often cross gender lines to communicate with our significant others.

Awareness of the difficulty of communicating across cultural divides is currently high in the United States. Race is one of the most troubling cultural divides in the United States, but it is only one of many. Violence against African Americans and other people of color, against homosexuals, against Native Americans, and against women of all races forms part of the backdrop of my study. The O. J. Simpson trial is only one of many recent incidents that graphically illustrates how deep the cultural divides run in the United States. Many blacks and whites have enormous difficulties understanding one another. Cases of sexual harassment graphically illustrate the divides between men and women. There has been a slight decrease in poverty rates in the last few years, but the income gap separating rich and poor has escalated dramatically. It is against this backdrop of racism, sexism, homophobia, ever-widening class differences, and a climate of pervasive mistrust and misunderstanding that I ask whether we can understand the aesthetic judgments of those who may seem, at least at first glance, quite different from ourselves. The United States is not the only place on this earth where divisions run deep, but if we learn to communicate better here, then there is hope for others facing deep cultural divisions.

Even while focusing on the situation of understanding across racial lines in the United States, I use a variety of figures out of the Western tradition to help me think about this problem. Immanuel Kant, Friedrich Nietzsche, Martin Heidegger, Theodor Adorno, Jacques Derrida, Toni Morrison, Davis, hooks, Collins, and West are the thinkers from whom I have learned the most about understanding aesthetic judgments. The first four may seem like strange choices for this project. Kant, Heidegger, and Adorno are particularly Eurocentric. Nietzsche, although often critical of Europe, is openly misogynistic and classist. Each of these four demonstrates, often graphically, an inability to cross cultural divides to understand others, and yet each has a positive contribution to make to this project. Kant is an important source for my optimism about the communicability of aesthetic judgments. The later Nietzsche—at times—is particularly insightful about the cultural embeddedness of art. Heidegger's notion of art as an opening up of a world and Adorno's analysis of the relationship between thought and aesthetics are also critical to my own thinking about the understanding of art. I have serious reservations about each of these thinkers' aesthetic theories, but I have learned a great deal from them. This is an attempt to build bridges across cultural divides, to promote conversation where little has taken place. Or, more precisely, this is an attempt by someone who has been schooled in traditional aesthetic theory to widen his field of vision. African-American thinkers have long been reading the canon of dead white males. Hooks notes that many African Americans have been influenced by European theorists such as Michel Foucault, Julia Kristeva, Derrida, and Jacques Lacan.[4] Clearly, the Frankfurt School has also been important to West as well as to Angela Davis, Lewis Gordon, and Lorenzo Simpson. Collins, hooks, and West do not only write about postmodernism. All three of them, even while often critical of some aspects of postmodernism, acknowledge that they are sympathetic to the notion of deconstruction and decentering.[5] Gordon is critical of postmodernism but grounds his critique in, among other traditions, a neo-marxism heavily indebted to the Frankfurt school.[6] African Americans have been reading and writing about these theorists; it is past time for white scholars to engage African-American thought more seriously.[7]

Once we acknowledge the shortcomings of the Western philosophic tradition, we can see that it contains useful tools to analyze the limits of our traditional notions. New paradigms of understanding are undoubtedly indebted to older ones. By training and birth I am an heir to Western aesthetic traditions; even my questioning of these traditions reveals my tethers to them. But in trying to understand African-American thought, Euro-Americans will, as West writes, learn a great deal about themselves:[8]

> Afro-American studies was never meant to be solely for Afro-Americans. . . . It was meant to try to redefine what it means to be human, what it means to be modern, what it means to be American, because people of African descent in this country are profoundly human, profoundly modern, profoundly American. And so to the degree to which they can see the riches that we have to offer as well as see our shortcomings, is the degree to which they can more fully understand the American experience.[9]

In reading and listening to others I am learning a great deal about my own notions of aesthetic experience.

I am interested in how we understand art and aesthetic judgments across cultural divides because such judgments are extremely important. Not just judgments about art, but all of our aesthetic judgments—be they about art, nature, or the way we arrange the places where we live—are some of the most important activities that humans engage in.[10] In the first place, art, particularly for oppressed people, is often a vital resource for the affirmation of self-worth. Hooks, for example, explains the role that art played in the lives of African Americans, particularly the role it played in affirming self-worth before the civil rights era. Art is also important because it tells us about ourselves. For more than one hundred years—at least since the impressionists—we in the West have known that a painting does not have to portray what is "really there." Even a "realistic portrait" can make someone look better or worse than he or she "really is." Like Adorno, I would say that, precisely because art never claims to tell the truth in a systematic way, it can at times be more truthful than those forms of knowledge that claim to tell us the truth. Art does not have the whole truth, but for this very reason, it can be insightful about many aspects of human life. A sonnet from Shakespeare can tell us more about love than any scientific explanation, or at least it tells us things that the "scientific" explanation cannot. Alice Walker and Toni Morrison write about human strength and weakness in a way that psychology—be it Freud or an article in a contemporary psychology journal—cannot. Of course, psychology can tell us other things that novels and poetry do not. Art tells us about ourselves and about others without the pretense that it is telling us the whole truth. It stretches and challenges the boundaries of our understanding and points to the limits of our more scientific ways of knowing. Whereas it is often assumed—mostly by non-scientists, ironically enough—that science claims to have truth, art's relationship to truth and reality has always been problematic. A more sophisticated understanding of science suggests that science offers us the power of repeatable quantifiable experimentation. It offers us the power of predictability, but a predictability within very narrowly prescribed limits. Morrison's *Paradise* helps me to think about the relationships between black men and black women. Morrison writes of love in a time when many black women seem overwhelmed by racism and sexism, but both Shakespeare and Morrison leave much of the process of interpreting to their readers. They set the stage and move the characters; and we muse about the meaning of it all. Art offers us a window onto that which we cannot quantify. But because it resists scientific explanation it is, at least in some ways, more difficult to understand and to discuss. Scientists are dedicated to making their results clear and verifiable. Artists often portray that which lies at the very limit of intelligibility. Art is an important way of understanding ourselves and our world, but it is also a difficult thing to understand across a cultural divide because it lacks the clarity and repeatability of scientific knowledge.

By "art" I mean a wide variety of cultural productions. I will not limit this discussion to the art that hangs on the walls of famous Western museums or the symphonies that are played in concert halls. The West is enthralled with the notion of the masterpiece. For many, myself included, this notion is problematic. I am suspicious that our notion of the masterpiece is shaped by the needs of an ever more commercialized art industry. In the age of the blockbuster show and galleries and museums that must survive in an intensely competitive capitalistic marketplace, the concept of the masterpiece, the notion of great art or even good art, is deeply intertwined with the necessity to make money. It is often difficult to believe that these characterizations of art can be anything other than marketing tools. Museums and galleries need the money that the display and sale of masterworks bring. In the United States museums usually only support art to which their corporate sponsors will not object.

Film is art, rap music and the dress of hip hop is art, the music played in blues shacks, the quilts of African-American women and the quilts made by my own grandmother are art. Art is dance, both Western and non-Western. To the extent that we take care in the arrangement of our hair and our manner of dress, we create artworks. And African masks that are not made to be put on walls but to be danced and touched and to be owned by the entire community—these too are art, as are the baskets of East Africa. Masks play much different roles in African societies than paintings play in our own. By calling non-Western objects and practices "art" I do not wish to force these things into traditional paradigms. In the meeting with other cultures our understanding of what art is is meaningfully enhanced. If I use this word "art" to describe certain objects from a non-Western society, it is with the intention of stretching and expanding my Western concept.

And yet the word "art," even in my expanded definition, is a very Western notion, and it will never do justice to all the things I want to talk about here. I want to expand the notion of art to include more of the everyday activities in the United States as well as the products of other non-Western cultures. But in so doing, I am inevitably shaping the phenomenon that I see, touch, read, and hear by my Western notion of art. In short, in trying to understand the other I will always to some extent be shaping that other by the Western critical apparatus that I bring to this project. This attempt to understand the other requires constant analyses of my self, not in an impossible effort to arrive at a mythical presuppositionless objective stance, but rather to explore and understand better the parameters of my presuppositions.

Art is found in the way that people arrange the spaces where they live and the things they hang on their walls. Bell hooks writes about how her grandmother valued the aesthetic in everyday life. Her grandmother was a poor African-American woman who lived in rural Kentucky. She was a quilt maker, and hooks reports that her grandmother also cared a great deal about how her house was arranged. She saw beauty in the colors around her. She braided tobacco leaves and hung them from her porch as a way of beautifying her house. Interestingly, hooks reports that some of her sisters remember their grandmother's house differently, as a place cluttered and not beautiful at all.

Not all art is interesting to all people. One might argue that many things can be called art, but not all of these things will touch all people, and some of these things may be judged to be of much higher quality than other things we may call art. I am interested in examining art that, to borrow from Heidegger, opens up a world. That is to say, artworks explode boundaries. Artworks help us to see the inadequacy of traditional ways of understanding the world. Obviously some of the "masterpieces" can surely do this, as can some of the works we find in those galleries that are currently flourishing in the marketplace. I do not exclude all traditional works of "great art" from this study, but rather I wish to open up our thinking about art to include works, as well as judgments, that have not been included in the canon.[11] In asking whether and to what extent we can understand artworks and aesthetic judgments that originate in cultures somewhat removed from us, I am interested not only in the "great works" exhibited in the accepted venues of high culture, although I am interested in them as well. I am most interested in the works and judgments that cultures and subcultures find to be particularly meaningful. And sometimes these are all the more meaningful given that they are not displayed in a manner that cuts them off from their audience. Quilts hung on walls are cut off from their use to warm us. We feel the warmth of a quilt used as a bedspread. The power of a mask is much greater when it is danced. Given my suspicion of masterpieces, when I use the term "aesthetic judgment," I am not referring to judgments of quality. I do not completely reject the application of judgments of quality to art, but given the way that such judgments have been used to marginalize art in the past, I am not yet ready to explore how judgments of quality can be assigned to art. This study concentrates on how it is possible to understand artworks and the interpretations that others have about art. By "aesthetic judgments" then I do not mean judgments of quality; instead I am referring to the way artworks have been interpreted.

The question of whether and to what extent we can understand art across cultural borders demands that we think about what it means to understand something. Specifically, it demands that we explore the relationship of feelings and understanding. It is one thing to understand a piece of art; it is another thing to feel something when seeing a piece of art. It is much easier to understand works of art or aesthetic judgments across cultural divides, and I am only arguing that cross-cultural understanding is possible. I am less certain that one can feel what someone else feels. "Do not tell me what I am feeling" is an injunction that few of us are willing to contest. And yet we do ask our friends, or pay our therapists, to help us clarify our feelings. It is clearly not as easy to understand another's feelings as it is to understand another's thoughts, but we can try to understand, I think, what someone else is feeling.

How do we go about understanding the art and the aesthetic judgments that come from someone different from ourselves? We should begin by assuming that we are not the experts and that we have a great deal to learn from others. Jean-Paul Sartre warns us that our imagination often tells us more about ourselves than others. To understand someone else's art, it is essential to study the person and the culture out of which the art comes. If we study the "life world" of that individual and group, then we will surely better understand the artwork.¹² Another useful strategy is to test our judgments by discussing them with others who have other perspectives. Most important, we must not assume that we know better. It is particularly difficult for philosophers to give up the hermeneutical prejudice that we understand more deeply and profoundly—that we understand the work better than the artist has understood it—but if we are to understand others across cultural divides the humility of an apprentice will be essential. In understanding the aesthetic judgments of others there is no shortcut. Such understanding requires the study of the worlds out of which the art comes, assuming that others understand these worlds better than we do. I do not want to say, however, that there are all-knowing masters who understand these artworks perfectly. Artists themselves have an important voice in understanding the art they create, but they do not have the final word. There are those who are masters at creating art, but the work itself always remains somewhat of an enigma, even to those who are closest to it. There are many important voices in the community out of which the art comes, usually the most important voices, but not the final ones. Some can understand better without anyone having absolute mastery. In short, I am proposing that in trying to understand art across cultural borders we consider ourselves apprentices who have given up the hope of finding all-knowing masters. There are many people from whom we can learn. Some people are better positioned to understand an artwork than others. Apprentices will see that they have a great deal to learn and will seek out those who can help them.

Whenever we are trying to understand that which comes from another cultural sphere, we should take heart from the fact that we all participate in a variety of cultural communities. Postcolonial studies and cultural studies have taught us that borders rarely cut as clearly and distinctly as we think they do.¹³ Certainly the cultural borders about which we most often speak—race, class, gender, ethnicity, and sexual orientation—are not as clearly delineated as our usage suggests. Our identities are always hybrids. We must cross borders every day to communicate with those with whom we share our lives. We must often cross gender borders to communicate with our spouses and generational borders to communicate with children and parents. In addition, there are other factors, particularly in aesthetics, that serve to separate us from each other. Art in general, and modern art in particular, is an acquired taste. How often do we find, for example, that our aesthetic judgments differ from the judgments of other members of our families, or our friends with whom we may share a racial or ethnic identity, or class, or gender? It is important to recognize the borders that separate us from each other, but if we are not careful, our recognition of difference can serve to overemphasize the differences between us and obscure the ways in which we can communicate across cultural divides. We should explore our differences, but our very real differences should not become excuses for our lack of communication; neither should our difficulties obscure the fact that we are constantly crossing borders and communicating with others. Communication across cultural divides is often difficult, but it is possible. In fact, we do it almost every time we enter into a conversation.

We will never understand the art of other cultures if we do not consider it. The hermeneutic process of interpretation can become a hermetic process. In the United States the art of people of color and the art of women often do not gain admission to the venues of high culture. The mainstream art world is, for the most part, dominated by white men. Often the exclusion of underrepresented groups is justified through a reference to quality.[14] The art of people outside the mainstream is said not to measure up to the high standards of the cultural institution. Unfortunately, the institutions that invariably seem to turn again and again to the art of white men never stop to ask themselves about the nature of their standards. Adrian Piper, an African-American woman who is an artist and a philosopher, reports that these critiques can be devastating for those excluded. Those victimized are being attacked in very private places in "their preferences, tastes, modes of self expression and self image. . . . When cultural racism succeeds in making its victims suppress, denigrate, or reject these means of cultural self-affirmation . . . it makes victims hate themselves."[15]

The exclusion of the underrepresented not only hurts the victims of prejudice, but it is also detrimental for the world of art. In the United States, we are seeing remarkable demographic changes. The number of Spanish-speaking people is rapidly rising. The number of Asian Americans is also increasing. There will be more women of color than white men living in the United States by the middle of the twenty-first century. If art—and let me quickly add that this is true for philosophy as well—does not speak of and to the concerns of these people, it will become ever more marginalized. Aestheticians and philosophers in general often believe themselves to have obtained universal knowledge. In retrospect, it is easy to see the gender and class biases that inform, for example, Aristotle's vision of the ideal state. We may be less aware of the cultural situatedness of our ideas of great art, and it is quite probable that we will be blind to some of the cultural baggage we carry in our critiques.

As we will see, many writers from underrepresented groups write about the importance of critical writings to the art of underrepresented people. Hooks, in particular, has suggested that these writings can help the artworks of underrepresented groups become more accessible to majority culture.[16] We can understand the aesthetic feelings of others, even when we are not moved as they are.

Chapter 1 uses bell hooks, Immanuel Kant, and Cornel West to explore the question of how cross-cultural understanding of art might be possible. I reject Kant's claim that aesthetics must be based on disinterested feelings. There are, however, two important resources for this study to be found in Kant. First, Kant's notion that aesthetic judgments are reflective rather than determinate suggests that they can be seen (even if Kant does not see them in this way) as built up out of an amalgamation of many factors. It is through the study of these diverse factors that we understand aesthetic judgments of others. Second, Kant suggests in a little-noticed passage in *The Critique of Judgment* that aesthetic judgment might also be grounded in the pleasure of communication. In section 41 of *The Critique of Judgment* Kant writes of this "empirical pleasure" derived from communicating with others. Although Kant ultimately rejects this source of aesthetic pleasure, I think that with this brief foray Kant is onto something. Hooks and West affirm that there is great pleasure in the communication of our aesthetic judgments and provide us with some further suggestions about how communication about aesthetic judgment across race and gender lines is more possible than Kant ever imagined. Hooks and West clearly believe that cross-cultural understanding of aesthetic judgment is possible. We can understand the aesthetic judgments of others not because, as Kant believed, aesthetic judgments are disinterested, but rather because we can understand something of the way that our interests permeate our aesthetic judgments.

Blues singers have always understood that their art comes out of their lives. Chapter 2 turns to the blues and to Nietzsche to investigate the social construction of art. Nietzsche's early theory of art (as enunciated in *The Birth of Tragedy*) suggests that great art arises out of two primordial drives and that the individual artist is little more than a conduit for these drives. The later Nietzsche, at times, claims that artistic creation is a product of one's physiology. To the extent that Nietzsche loses sight of the social embeddedness of art, he can't sing the blues. But in his later writings he often sees the artist as the paradigmatic example of one who creates his or her own values as opposed to following the herd. This Nietzsche believes that it is through analysis—through a genealogical study of one's own time—that one creates his values. The later Nietzsche is in a constant dialogue with European (and a few Asian) thinkers, past and present. Although Nietzsche's rhetoric may sometimes suggest that he is a lonely thinker cut off from all society, it is through interactions with others that his philosophy and his art arise. This is the bluesy Nietzsche. This is the Nietzsche who recognizes that his thought is an extensive interaction with the cultural icons of Western civilization. By his practice, if not always in his rhetoric, Nietzsche presents us with a graphic example of the social nature of creation that arises once the belief in primordial drives has subsided. In short, once he has undermined all belief in absolutes, philosophy and aesthetics can be nothing other than an extended conversation with social constructs. Nietzsche continually emphasizes the importance of the social world in the construction and understanding of reality; I am therefore hopeful that if we spend time investigating the worlds out of which art and aesthetic judgments come, we will be able to understand these works and judgments. Unlike Nietzsche, blues singers are *always* aware that the inspiration for their art comes from their social reality. Comparing Angela Davis's interpretation of blues and Nietzsche's visions of artistic creation, I argue that Davis is unambiguous about the social origins of art. At times, Nietzsche recognizes that artistic creation is embedded in social reality, but at other times he does not. As Davis shows in *Blues Legacies and Black Feminism,* these singers never lose sight of how art is embedded in social life.[17]

Having argued that we can understand the art of others and that art's social embeddedness is the key to understanding it, in chapter 3 I explore the relationship between an artwork and the social world. Hooks charges that many white critics, writing about Jean-Michel Basquiat, have failed to understand how much of his work is shaped by the suffering he felt as a person of color living in a racist society. Basquiat was a Haitian-American artist who became internationally known at a very young age. During his short life he achieved critical and financial success. He died of a heroin overdose before reaching the age of thirty. Hooks argues that white critics often focus on Basquiat's relationship to Andy Warhol and do not recognize the extent to which his work expresses the pain he felt as a result of racism.

I purpose apprenticeship as one strategy to help us avoid misunderstanding and misappropriating the art and aesthetic judgments of others. I am not suggesting that there are omniscient masters who can tell us all we need to know to master the art of other cultures. I am, instead, advocating apprenticeship as an antidote to the philosophical arrogance that believes itself capable of understanding the artwork and of rendering aesthetic judgments better than the artist and those who know the worlds of the artist best. Apprentices recognize that they have a great deal to learn. They approach their study with the humility born of an understanding of how much they do not know.

In chapter 3 I argue that Heidegger supplies us with an important understanding of an artwork. I examine Heidegger's attempt to understand art as an opening up of a world. As much as I am attracted to this understanding of art, Heidegger's essay graphically illustrates some of the problems inherent in this view of art. Heidegger, as Meyer Shapiro shows, flagrantly misappropriates Van Gogh in his essay "On the Origin of the Artwork." In this essay, Heidegger explains how a Van Gogh painting of a pair of shoes opens up a German peasant woman's world. Starting from this painting, Heidegger goes on to talk about German peasant life. But Shapiro argues that in fact the shoes in question were not peasant shoes but rather the shoes of Van Gogh himself, who was at this time a city dweller. Shapiro is certainly right about the narrow point that Heidegger's equation of the painting of the shoes with a German peasant woman's shoes constitutes, to use Derrida's term, a "hijacking." But Heidegger's larger point—that artworks open up worlds—not only, in my opinion, leads to a richer understanding of art, but it also leads quite naturally to the conclusion that to understand an artwork we must explore the world out of which the artwork originates. Derrida's careful analysis of the Heidegger-Shapiro debate gives us a wonderful example of apprenticeship. Derrida's analysis opens up the worlds of the debate between Heidegger and Shapiro. He attentively analyzes Heidegger's and Shapiro's texts, as well as several of Van Gogh's paintings, and digs deeply into the historical and personal stories that lie behind the scholarly writings of Heidegger and Shapiro. It is hard to say what does or does not belong to the world of this painting. When is the "opening" of an artwork merely the excuse for the interpreter to rehash his or her familiar convictions? As rich as his analysis is, at some point, it seems that Derrida's analysis takes us rather far afield of Van Gogh's painting and even the Heidegger-Shapiro debate itself. The truth of art is not found in repeatable experimentally fixed results. It happens, Heidegger would say, in the opening. I am inclined to agree that there is an important distinction between art and science. The notion of an opening is perhaps one of the most insightful ways to think about art, but I am nonetheless troubled by how easily this way of approaching the art of others can lead us to falsifying appropriations. There is no way to ensure that our interpretations of others are attentive to others, but my invocation of apprenticeship is suggested as a strategic intervention. It does not guarantee that the artwork will be "correctly" understood.

The relationship between art and thought is difficult to define. Chapter 4 explores the relationship between art and thought, a relationship that is notoriously difficult to understand. Even though Adorno, particularly in his treatment of jazz, is the prototypical Eurocentric thinker, he has thought more deeply about the relationship between thought and art than any other Western philosopher. Moreover, Adorno is more intimately acquainted with Western art than most other philosophers. He provides us, then, with the opportunity to investigate the extent to which it is possible to understand art at all. Furthermore, he reminds us of the ways in which art is commodified and subverted by the culture industry.

Adorno argues that art can and should be disruptive. It is not fully accessible to the rational but not entirely divorced from it, either. Art cries out for interpretation. We can understand art, even art that seems very foreign to us, even if we do not understand it completely. But what do we say when a perceptive critic like Adorno turns toward an art that many of us esteem—namely jazz—and derides it as "perennial fashion"? What if the study of someone else's art leads the critic to dismiss it? I am not saying that the understanding of one another's art will lead us all to feel the same way about art. Nor will the understanding of each other's art lead us all to a similar evaluation of the work of art. Understanding does not mean that we will like or even respect a work or genre of art. Even within what may appear to some outside observers as heterogenous communities, people feel about and evaluate artworks very differently. There is not a unitary black perspective on the work of Horace Pippen, nor a unitary white perspective on the work of Jackson Pollock. But Adorno's comments on jazz do not, in my opinion, constitute an understanding of jazz. Adorno dismisses jazz—or more precisely appropriates jazz to serve as an example of corrupt bourgeois culture—without having evidenced that he ever really tried to understand it. In short, I believe it is possible to take much of what Adorno wrote about art and apply it with more sensitivity to the demands that cross-cultural understanding entails.

Concluding with an examination of the relationship between art and politics, in chapter 5 I argue that not only is politics the legitimate stuff of art, but art will almost always be grappling with the social and political realities of its day. Indeed the choice to make art dealing with the lives of women and African Americans is a political decision, as is the choice to make art about white males. The notion of the masterpiece is often used in the commerce of art. It can divert our attention from art outside the mainstream. There is a great deal of important art that exists outside the venues of high culture. As I have already said, I am suspicious of art that is closely tied to the capitalist marketplace. Art that opens up a world will not necessarily be art that is commercially successful. This chapter explores the politics of interpretation and the politics surrounding the control of images. It also examines the controversy involving John Ahearn, a white artist, who has lived and worked for many years in the South Bronx. Ahearn is a sculptor who often works on the sidewalk in front of his apartment making casts of the faces of people who live in his adopted South Bronx neighborhood—one of the most economically distressed places in the United States. Deeply concerned about his relationships with those whom he portrays, he makes two casts and gives one of them to the person portrayed. The other cast can sell for thousands of dollars in Soho galleries. Ahearn wished to memorialize three people he knew from his neighborhood by erecting bronze statues of them in a square a few bocks from where he lives. He made statues of a thirty-three-year-old Latino man with his pitbull, a fourteen-year-old African-American teenager on her roller skates, and a twenty-something African-American with a "boom box." Those portrayed like the sculptures, but some middle-class Latinos and African Americans wanted the statues removed. They wanted statues of prominent African-American and Latino heroes. Ahearn voluntarily removed the statues, at his own expense, five days after he had erected them.

Although I have argued that there are no final authorities on either the interpretation or the use of images, we should exercise caution and humility in both areas. If we engage in serious and prolonged discussions about art with others, there will be disagreements. To understand each other does not mean that we will always agree with each other, nor does it mean that we will always agree about the use of images. Our disagreements will often be painful, but they will also provide us with opportunities to gain new perspectives on ourselves and others.

I am—it is obvious, is it not?—deeply concerned about cross-cultural understanding in general and our ability to understand art across cultures in particular. It is not so difficult, I think, to understand *Wissenschaften*—scientific knowledge in the broadest sense—across cultural borders. The wonder, beauty, and importance of art is its ability to touch those parts of our existence that we know the *Wissenschaften* were never meant to reach. This is not a disinterested treatise designed to dissect these issues with scholarly indifference to the outcome. Understanding the aesthetic judgments of others is difficult, and yet I want to encourage people to try. In so doing we will learn a great deal about ourselves as well.

NOTES

1. I should perhaps pay more attention to the notion of the quality of the artwork. Adrian Piper argues that the notion of quality is important at this historical moment because women and people of color are beginning to be recognized as producing objects of quality. The judgment that a work has "objective quality" can be empowering to the artist. It is not the claims about quality, but the limitation of quality to Western art, that Piper finds problematic. See Adrian Piper, *Out of Order, Out of Sight*, vol. 2 of *Selected Writings in Art Criticism 1967–1992* (Cambridge: MIT Press, 1996), 198.

2. W. E. B. Du Bois, *The Souls of Black Folks* (New York: Bantam, 1989). He makes this claim in both "The Forethought" and chapter 2, "On the Dawn of Freedom."

3. Not that the biology/culture distinction is as clear as we generally tend to believe. Butler has problematized this distinction in interesting ways in *Gender Trouble*. At least since Hegel we have understood that it is never easy to isolate a concept and that concepts have a way of implying their opposites. Since Nietzsche, however, we have seen that there is no reason to hold back from employing problematic notions. Nietzsche urged us not to worry about the truth content of notions but rather how notions are useful or even necessary for life. See Judith Butler, *Gender Trouble*, 2d ed. (New York: Routledge, 1999).

4. bell hooks and Cornel West, *Breaking Bread: Insurgent Black Intellectual Life* (Boston: South End Press, 1991), 35.

5. See, for example, Patricia Hill Collins, *Fighting Words: Black Women and the Search for Social Justice* (Minneapolis: University of Minnesota Press, 1998), in particular chapter 4, "What's Going On? Black Feminist Thought and the Politics of Postmodernism." For one of the places where hooks writes about postmodernism, see bell hooks, *Yearnings: Race, Gender and Cultural Politics* (Boston: South End Press, 1990), in particular "The Politics of Radical Black Subjectivity" and "Postmodern Blackness." See also bell hooks and Cornel West, *Breaking Bread: Insurgent Black Intellectual Life* (Boston: South End Press, 1991).

6. See Lewis Gordon, *Her Majesty's Other Children: Sketches of Racism from a Neocolonial Age* (Lanham, Md.: Rowman & Littlefield, 1997), in particular chapter 5, "Uses and Abuses of Blackness: Postmodernism, Conservatism, Ideology," 89–114.

7. Some white scholars are doing this. See, for example, Cynthia Willet's book *Maternal Ethics and Other Slave Moralities* (New York: Routledge, 1995), and Cynthia Willet, ed., *Theorizing Multiculturalism* (Maldwell, Mass.: Blackwell, 1998). See also Robert Bernasconi, ed., *Race* (Maldwell, Mass.: Blackwell, 2001) and Robert Bernasconi and Tommy Lott, *The Idea of Race* (Indianapolis, Ind.: Hackett, 2000).

8. hooks and West, *Breaking Bread*, 32.

9. Ibid., 32–33.

10. Paul Taylor argues, and I think he is right, that we do not need to limit the study of aesthetic judgments to the judgments we make about artworks. He discusses beauty in the context of cultural criticism, or more specifically, beauty in the context of black hair styles. See Paul Taylor, "Malcolm's Conk and Danto's Colors; or, Four Logical Petitions Concerning Race, Beauty, and Aesthetics," *Journal of Aesthetics and Art Criticism* 57, no. 1 (1999): 16–20.

11. I am impressed with Crispin Sartwell's *The Art of Living: Aesthetics of the Ordinary in World Spiritual Traditions* (Albany: State University of New York Press, 1995). Like Sartwell I want to continue to use Western notions such as "Art" to think about cultural productions from different cultures. I am also attempting to expand our notion of art and to understand experiences as art that are not a part of museum culture. I do not, however, want to focus exclusively on nontraditional arts. Samuel Beckett, William Faulkner, Toni Morrison, and Jean-Michel Basquiat are examples of mainstream artists whose work speaks powerfully to me and many others. I agree with Sartwell that there is much art to be found in our every-

day experiences, but then some of everyday life—Sartwell mentions that a well-crafted TV commercial can be thought of as art—seems so much in the service of consumer society that it has attained a level of false consciousness. I must admit that I will be hard pressed to delineate with any precision what is or is not art.

12. The notion of apprenticeship is borrowed from Elizabeth Spelman's *Inessential Woman* (Boston: Beacon Press, 1988), especially 180–82. She has, in turn, taken it from Jean-Paul Sartre's early work *Psychology of Imagination* (Secaucus, N.J.: Citadel Press, n.d.).

13. See, for example, Kwame Anthony Appiah, *In My Father's House: Africa in the Philosophy of Culture* (New York: Oxford University Press, 1992).

14. See, for example, Lucy Lippard's *Mixed Blessings* (New York: Pantheon, 1990), 7.

15. Ibid.

16. By stressing the variety of worlds in which we live, I am in partial agreement with Nelson Goodman's claim that worlds are "made as much as found" and that much of knowing is analogous to finding the piece of a jigsaw puzzle that fits as opposed to thinking of knowing as finding the truth. My analysis differs from his in giving much more attention to the role cultural factors play in the construction of the worlds we inhabit. See Nelson Goodman, *Ways of Worldmaking* (Indianapolis, Ind.: Hackett, 1978), 21.

17. Angela Davis, *Blues Legacies and Black Feminism: Gertrude "Ma" Rainey, Bessie Smith, and Billie Holiday* (New York: Pantheon Books, 1998).

1

UNDERSTANDING AESTHETIC JUDGMENTS ACROSS CULTURAL BORDERS

Today, particularly in the United States, we are often uneasy about how to understand art and aesthetic judgments made by those whose gender, race, class, ethnicity, or national origin differs from our own.[1] This "other" is, so the argument goes, too different for "us" to understand. Even those who do not explicitly maintain that cross-cultural understanding is impossible often make little effort to engage seriously aesthetic judgments that spring from those whose experiences are different from their own. Aesthetic understanding across cultural divides is difficult but possible. It requires us to study the worlds out of which this art comes and to engage in conversation with one another. Two extremes are to be avoided. There is not an unbridgeable gap in understanding, but neither are the other's aesthetic judgments readily accessible. The understanding of aesthetic judgments is rarely easy. No one can speak with final authority in aesthetic matters—not artists, not critics, not the community that spawns an artwork, not the present age, nor an age to come, and certainly not the philosopher. It is foolish to ignore any of the viewpoints accessible to us, but, particularly when crossing cultural borders into poorly known terrain, we should exercise extreme caution about our ability to understand others better than they understand themselves. We will not understand very much at all if we do not leave behind our assumptions of superior knowledge. To understand each other across cultural divides, we must leave our comfort zones and become students of the many worlds out of which each artwork arises.

Kant claims that aesthetic judgments are grounded in the feelings of individuals and yet are universal.[2] Close readers have noted the limited nature of Kant's conception of universality. Kant uses Native Americans to illustrate the difference between beauty and charm and asserts that they are rarely—if ever—capable of recognizing beauty.[3] Kant claims that aesthetic judgments are universal, but he also believes that Native Americans and many others are incapable of detaching themselves from charm and, therefore, are incapable of experiencing beauty. Even if the mature Kant—he was well into his eighties when he published *The Critique of Judgment*—made fewer wholesale generalizations about upper-class women and blacks than he did in his much earlier essay, *Observations on the Feeling of the Beautiful and Sublime*, it is clear that he did not really believe that all people would share the same aesthetic judgments. In many ways, Kant is a paradigmatic example of a tendency among Western philosophers to believe that they can understand others better than those others understand themselves.[4]

I argue that aesthetic judgments are always interested and yet communicable. The key to understanding is to analyze carefully the ways in which interest functions in our own judgments as well as in the judgments of others. As I dissect Kant's claim to have found the basis for subjective universal aesthetic judgments, we will see that Kant himself has great difficulties trying to establish the subjective disinterested universality of aesthetic judgments. I argue, with bell hooks and Cornel West and against Kant, that aesthetic judgments are inherently interested and that an examination of Kant will show us how interested his pretensions to disinterestedness are.

But for me Kant is not only an example of the pitfalls of cross-cultural communication. As limited as Kant's notion of universality is, it is important to recognize his concern for the communication of aesthetic judgments. This concern is one of the central motivations that leads him to formulate the notion of disinterested aesthetic judgments.[5] Writing against those who believe that enigmatic genius is at the root of all great art, Kant argues that "authentic genius sought universality."[6] Kant even argues at one point in *The Critique of Judgment* that aesthetic judgments, because they are based on feelings, have more of a right to be labeled *sensus communis* than do judgments of reason.[7] The key to universal understanding in matters of taste, according to Kant, is that judgments of taste, when free of all interest, will be universally shared.

Most important, there is a suggestion in *The Critique of Judgment* about how we might understand aesthetic judgments that has received little attention. In section 41, "On the Empirical Interest in the Beautiful," Kant writes about the possibility of an empirical aesthetic where aesthetic pleasure would arise from talking with each other. Here he argues that aesthetic pleasure might not only come from our immediate disinterested feelings, but that it also could arise out of our discussions about the beautiful. I too believe that discussion has an important role to play in the understanding of aesthetic judgments, particularly when we are trying to understand aesthetic judgments across cultural borders. At the same time, I recognize that even though discussions may help us to better *understand* one another, this does not always mean that we will all *feel* the same way.

There is a second way in which Kant's aesthetics help us to envision how cross-cultural aesthetic understanding is possible. His claim that aesthetic judgments are reflective as opposed to determinate helps us to envision how aesthetic judgments are built out of an aggregate of our interests: race, class, and sexual orientation, for example. Kant insists that aesthetic judgment begins with particulars and then seeks its universal. Reflective judgment helps us to conceptualize the interested nature of aesthetic judgment.

Turning to hooks and West, we see that they argue that cross-cultural understandings of art are not merely possible but in some sense inevitable. In writing about the art of African-American painter Horace Pippen, West imports categories from Ralph Waldo Emerson and John Dewey. Although Emerson, Pippen, and Dewey are separated by temporal and racial differences, class issues concern all three. West criticizes those who group black artists together merely because they are black, not recognizing the vast differences in their work. To focus exclusively on race is as limiting as excluding race from aesthetic discussions. Hooks argues that those who share race, class, gender, and even family affiliations often have very different aesthetic tastes. I am not arguing that communication across such cultural boundaries is easy, nor that our understanding is definitive. But understanding is made easier because we already contain many cultural identities within ourselves.[9] It may seem odd to suggest that Kant, West, and hooks taken together will provide us with important insights into how we understand each other's aesthetic judgments. But then again, I am interested in promoting conversation and understanding where little of either has taken place. To understand one another does not mean that everyone will agree. Indeed, we learn from one another and understand each other through both agreements and disagreements.

DISINTERESTED AESTHETIC JUDGMENTS?

According to Kant, judgments of taste are based on disinterested feelings of pleasure and displeasure that arise freely in the subject. Judgments of taste are "subjective" because they are based on feelings rather than cognition. The broad claim that beauty resides in the viewer as opposed to residing directly in the object seems more true the more we know about others whose experiences differ radically from our own. At the same time, Kant writes that the feelings that form the basis of judgments of beauty are "universal" (*allgemein*), although as we have already noted, there are many people who are not included in Kant's universality.

Crucial for his theory of beauty is the distinction between the agreeable (*das Angenehme*) and the beautiful (*das Schöne*). The judgment that something is agreeable does not demand universal agreement. It is both subjective and individual. Kant also writes that the liking associated with the agreeable is "based entirely on sensation" (C3, §4). Most important, the pleasure that originates in the agreeable is interested pleasure; that is to say, the agreeable produces a desire in us.[9] This distinction between disinterested and interested pleasure most clearly delineates the beautiful from the agreeable. The agreeable is that which satisfies one (*ihn vergnügt*), whereas the beautiful is that which merely pleases one (*ihm bloss gefällt*) (C3, §5).

Kant gives a number of examples to illustrate this point. One might say that sparkling wine from the Canary Islands is agreeable, but one should say that this wine is "agreeable for me" (C3, §7). One person finds the color violet "soft and lovely," whereas another person finds it dead and faded; one person loves wind instruments while another loves strings.[10] In questions concerning the agreeable it is foolish to argue about who is right, for in the realm of the agreeable "everyone has their [sic] own taste" (Ibid.).

But with questions of beauty things are different. For Kant, to judge something as beautiful means not only that it is beautiful for me, but that it also demands universal assent. This universality is not based on concepts since, according to Kant, there is no direct connection between concepts and feelings. The pleasure that arises from beauty is therefore a pleasure that originates in shared feelings.

Kant rarely argues for the universality of judgments of beauty. He assumes that judgments of beauty must be universal and then attempts to explain their universality. In the second moment of "The Analytic of the Beautiful" (§§6–9), there are numerous examples of Kant making recourse to common knowledge or to universal knowledge to justify the universality of beauty.[11] For example, Kant writes, *"That about which everyone is conscious* is that the liking (associated with the beautiful) is itself without interest—this liking cannot be otherwise judged for it must contain the ground for the liking of everyone" (C3, §6, emphasis added). Kant also gives a second justification for the universality of judgments of beauty. He says that the liking associated with the beautiful must be universal because it is not based on a private condition or individual whim. That there could be something between a universal and a private condition—for example a group preference—is an all-important possibility that Kant does not consider. Kant also writes that it would be ridiculous to say that something is beautiful for me. Something is not beautiful, Kant goes on to say, when it is only beautiful for one individual (C3, §7). To reduce beauty to the taste of an individual would mean "there is no such thing as taste; that is, there is no aesthetic judgment that could make a justifiable claim to universal assent" (C3, §7).

But the universality of assent to which Kant is referring is more limited than at first appears, and this becomes obvious when we examine the references *The Critique of Judgment* makes to, and the use it makes of, "exotic" peoples. Kant makes use of these "exotic natives"—he knew of these people, it seems, primarily through travel books—to illustrate his claims about the "universality" of aesthetic judgments and their limits. Most of us are no longer comfortable with this strategy. In section 2, Kant writes that Iroquois visiting Paris liked nothing better than the eating houses. The story seems to illustrate, for Kant, an inability to go beyond the charms of the appetite to an appreciation of the beautiful architecture of Paris.

In section 41, Kant again uses the Iroquois and the Carib to explain the difference between beauty and charm.[12] Their body paintings and their use of shells and brightly colored feathers are not beautiful, but only charming.[13] It is only in the shape of their canoes and of their clothes that beauty is achieved. Kant uses these people to delineate the difference between those who are capable of disinterested aesthetic judgments and those who judge only with their appetites.

In comparison to the "primitive," Kant asserts his own normative centrality. He and other northern European men can appreciate the beauty of Parisian buildings—even if, like Kant, they have never been there. They are also not involved in the frivolous practice of adorning their clothes with feathers. They can transcend charm and see "universal" beauty. They are capable of disinterested "universal" aesthetic judgment, but the exotic native is not. In an age-old philosophical trope, Kant characterizes the "primitive" as one who is ruled by his appetites, a servant of pleasure, incapable of experiencing disinterested beauty. But does not Kant's own interest—we might even call it Kant's passion—for delimiting the realm of reason evidence a similarly interested spirit? Is not Kant fascinated, even captivated, by the study of reason and its limits—perhaps a strange desire to our way of thinking, but a desire nonetheless? And might we not say that all aesthetics comes down to understanding our partiality and how it is that coming from the many different cultural spheres we inhabit, we feel very strongly about certain things and are less moved by other things? Moreover, if we invest the time and the effort to study the worlds out of which others come, may we understand something of the other's' aesthetic attachments even if we do not feel as they do? But I am getting ahead of myself here. Let us return to Kant.

PURPOSIVENESS AND REFLECTIVE JUDGMENT

Purposiveness provides the key, in Kant's aesthetics, to the "universality" of subjective feelings of beauty.[14] But it is less than clear exactly how purposiveness ensures universality. Part of the problem arises out of the changes that *The Critique of Judgment* underwent in the course of its composition.[15] I follow Giorgio Tonelli's suggestion that *The Critique of Judgment* was composed in the following order: (1) The Analytic of the Beautiful, (2) The Deduction of Pure Aesthetic Judgments, (3) The Dialectic of Aesthetic Judgment, (4) First Introduction, (5) Analytic of the Sublime, (6) Critique of Teleological Judgment, (7) (second) Introduction and Preface. Tonelli argues that one should not look for a unitary concept of purposiveness but rather should try to understand the development that the term undergoes within *The Critique of Judgment*.

In "The Analytic of the Beautiful" (the earliest section of *The Critique of Judgment*), Kant writes that beauty depends neither on the use of an object nor on its perfection (*Vollkommenheit*) (C3, §15).[16] That beauty is not a function of an object's usefulness seems readily apparent to Kant, and he dismisses this possibility quickly. The question of whether beauty is related to an object's perfection is more contentious, and he devotes more space to it. He writes that several renowned philosophers have believed perfection and beauty were one and the same. He, however, insists that because a judgment of taste is based on feelings, it cannot be determined by a concept.

This purposiveness that grounds judgments of taste is not the purposiveness of any empirical object. Kant refers to this purposiveness as a "purposiveness without a purpose" (*Zweckmäßigkeit ohne Zweck*). Despite the development in this concept there is, from the very beginning of the Third Critique to the end, a broad consensus that beauty's universality is a result of a "purposiveness without a purpose." Kant remains convinced that a disinterested pleasure arises when an object evokes in us a sense of the interrelatedness of our cognitive powers. This pleasure, Kant believes, is the origin of the feeling of beauty. But the descriptions of why and how this purposiveness without a purpose incites feelings of beauty vary.

Kant first introduces this strange sounding locution, which reappears in many places from the first to the last discussions of purposiveness, by saying that it is purposiveness according to form (*der Form nach*). Zammito argues that here purposiveness involves a "figurative use of language."[17] It refers to the fact that aesthetic judgments are based on the appearance of design, but there is no assurance that this design actually exists. Kant illustrates this notion of purity of form further in the "Elucidation through Examples" (C3, §14). Purity of form is not found in a mere impression (*Empfindung*) but rather in the "formal determination of the unity of a manifold" (C3, §14).[18]

Kant writes that the purpose that serves as the ground for a judgment of taste can be neither subjective nor objective. In claiming that it is not subjective, Kant means that beauty is not to be judged by whether the object serves some subjective purpose. Neither is the purpose that determines aesthetic judgments objective in the sense that Kant believes judgments about the good can be objective. It is rather a purpose that has only to do with "the relationship of the presentational powers (*die Vorstellungkräfte*) to each other" (C3, §11). Aesthetic liking is "merely contemplative" and is without direct interest in the object: "The consciousness of the merely formal purposiveness in the play of the cognitive powers of the subject in a representation through which an object is given is liking itself" (C3, §12). In other words, aesthetic liking arises out of the interplay of our cognitive powers, not directly out of our perception of the object. Some objects bring about in us an awareness of the purposiveness evidenced in the workings of our cognitive powers. These objects precipitate an enlivening (*Belebung*) of our cognitive powers. This enlivening makes us want to linger in our contemplation of the beautiful. This is the origin of our aesthetic feelings. This liking cannot originate out of an individual representation but rather necessarily originates out of the relationships between our many representational powers.

Kant's belief that the source of our feelings is not in the object but rather in the relationship of our cognitive powers causes him to reject what he calls the "standard idea of beauty." Given a thousand men, Kant writes that it would be possible to calculate the average height, head, or nose, but this would only give us the standard idea of beauty. He admits that this standard idea would differ for Europeans, Chinese, and Negroes. Such a standard idea of beauty is in no way the entire "archetype of beauty." It can have no specific characteristics because these would contradict the standard idea. Such a standard would be merely correct according to the ideal of the schools (C3, §17). Kant is obviously aware that people from different cultures may have different ideas of beauty, but he believes that true beauty is seen only when one rises above the standard set by a particular culture and feels the purposiveness in the play of the cognitive powers. Kant assumes that the delight that he feels at the sudden "discovery" of the coherence of nature's laws is the only legitimate foundation for the "universality" of beauty.

The Critique of Judgment is an impressive work in many ways. It remains remarkably contemporary in its insistence that aesthetic judgments are based on feelings and not on logic. But is there such a thing as a disinterested feeling? Kant's attempt to find the source for aesthetic judgments in the feelings arising out of the interplay of our cognitive powers is deeply intertwined with his lifelong goal of achieving a grand system linking moral and cognitive reason. Kant believed that he found in the critique of aesthetic judgment the linchpin for his life work; surely this reflects the highest interest of a great metaphysician. Kant also does not want to give up on the notion of universal aesthetic judgments, for he fears this would lead, among other things, to an inability to communicate with each other about aesthetic matters.

UNIVERSALITY AND REFLECTIVE JUDGMENT

In the course of writing his critique of aesthetic judgments, Kant formulates a key insight, namely that aesthetic judgments are reflective and not determinate. This notion of reflective judgment can help us, I believe, to understand how, in the absence of universal aesthetic judgments, we can still understand each other across cultural divides. Kant assumes from the very beginning of the Third Critique that judgments of beauty have universal validity, but his explanation for their universality is substantially amended when he introduces the notion of reflective judgment.[19] It is in the Introductions—written after much of the book had been completed—that reflective and determinate judgments are explicitly distinguished and reflective judgment's relationship to our disinterested feelings of liking is most clearly presented.[20] Judgment, in general, is the capacity to subsume the particular under a general law. If the general principle is given, then the judgment is determinative. If, however, the particular is given and we must seek the universal, then Kant calls this reflective judgment (C3, "Introduction," §IV). There is much about Kant's conception of beauty that I question, but this insight that judgments of beauty are reflective—that is, built out of the particular and seeking the universal—is one of the key elements of Kant's thought onto which I hold fast. Aesthetic judgments are often spontaneous, but when we try to understand our aesthetic judgments or the judgments of others, we must carefully explore the myriad individual factors that have gone into the formation of these judgments.

Reflective judgment, Kant writes, is a transcendental principle because it is concerned with possible experience rather than experience itself (C3, "Introduction," §V). Kant claims that reflective judgment cannot find its law in experience. Rather, reflective judgment gives itself this law that makes possible the systematization of nature. The purposiveness of nature is not discovered through often-repeated phrases such as "Nature takes the shortest way" or "Nature does not make leaps either in the path of its changes or in the combination of its various forms" (C3, "Introduction," §V). Reflective judgment makes it possible for us to apprehend nature as a "coherent experience." Without the assumption of the purposiveness of nature it would be impossible to speak of the order of nature. As Rudolf Makkreel writes, aesthetic forms suggest "the overall systematic structure of the world. . . . Both in the case of natural and artificial beauty, the purposiveness felt refers to the overall order of our experience."[21] In other words, Kant does not believe that aesthetic judgments can ever be universal unless they are transcendentally oriented.[22] Aesthetic judgments are not to be found through empirical research; rather, they are to be discovered through reference to our ability to understand nature.

After describing the necessary but reflective nature of aesthetic judgments in section 5 of the Introduction, Kant explains how aesthetic judgments are connected with the feelings of pleasure and displeasure in sections 6 and 7. In section 6 Kant claims that the feeling of liking (*Lust*) is a priori and universal. This universality is produced out of the "relationship of an object to our capacities for knowledge (*Erkenntnisvermögen*)" (C3, "Introduction," §VI). The universality of aesthetic judgments is not related to our capacity for desire and, therefore, is completely divorced from all practical or moral purposiveness of nature (*sich von aller praktischen Zweckmäßigkeit der Natur gänzlich unterscheidet*).[23] Aesthetic feelings are also unrelated, according to Kant, to the work of the understanding; that is to say, the feeling of the beautiful does not arise when perceptions are synthesized under the categories of the understanding.

Beauty is, rather, the product of the discovery of the unity of two or more empirically heterogeneous laws of nature under a basic principle (*unter einem sie beide befassenden Prinzip der Grund*). When this happens, we experience a liking that endures even if we already know the object. The basis for judgments of beauty is, for Kant, not the object itself but rather the object's ability to evoke the systematic unity of nature's laws.

The purposiveness that grounds aesthetic judgment must be a reflective principle, according to Kant, because it is grounded in the subject. To judge a thing as purposive does not say anything about the object, or as Kant puts it, "through purposiveness I know nothing of the object of representation" (C3, "Introduction," §VII). According to Kant, we perceive objects without necessarily evoking purposiveness. It is only when liking accompanies perception that we call an object purposive.

Kant's explanation of exactly how reflective judgment produces the liking that arises in aesthetic pleasure is less than clear. Section VII of the second Introduction adds to section VI by discussing the role of the imagination in the production of our feelings of beauty. The discussion is very dense and complex, even by Kant's standards. In trying to understand this discussion in particular and the relationship of reflective judgment and purposiveness in general, there are several things worth noting. First, Kant has already claimed that purposiveness is the key to aesthetic liking in the earliest sections of *The Critique of Judgment,* and he does so without recourse to the notion of reflective judgment. Second, the vocabulary changes slightly in this Introduction. Although there is some mention of *Lust,* the "Analytic of the Beautiful" refers overwhelmingly to *Wohlgefallen* as the feeling that gives rise to judgments of beauty. Section VII of the Introduction, on the other hand, refers to *Lust* as the feeling at the origin of beauty. Third, in the Introduction imagination plays a crucial role in explaining how reflective judgment functions in the production of aesthetic liking. Imagination is mentioned in the "Analytic of the Beautiful," but only briefly.[24]

Kant writes that aesthetic liking comes about through our *"blossen Auffassung* (apprehension) [mere apprehension] of the form of an object" (C3, "Introduction, §VII). It is not the product of a concept. This liking is necessarily traceable to the subject and is nothing other than the result of the object's being commensurate with our cognitive capacities (Ibid.). We discover this commensurability through reflective, not determinative, judgment.

Unlike what he states in the "Analytic of the Beautiful," in the Introduction Kant writes that it is the imagination that apprehends the form of the object in aesthetic judgments. Imagination could never apprehend these forms if reflective judgment did not compare the forms with its ability to refer intuitions to concepts. If in this comparison the imagination and understanding are found to be in harmony, a feeling of pleasure is produced and reflective judgment considers the object as purposive. The pleasure is not created by the concept directly. It is found, rather, merely in the form the object takes for reflection.[25] It is only the lawful character in the empirical use of the judgment in the subject in general (the unity of imagination with understanding) that agrees with the representation of the object in reflection whose conditions are valid a priori. And because this agreement is accidental, it causes a representation of purposiveness in the object in relation to the cognitive powers of the subject. Kant's insistence that it is the form and not the content of the object that gives rise to our feelings of pleasure reinforces his insistence upon the disinterested nature of beauty's pleasure. One imagines that form might be described by disinterested mathematical formulae, whereas content inevitably conjures up images of "messy" emotional involvement. But against Kant, I do not believe that our immediate reactions to form are the only thing that we are sure to share universally. But then, unlike Kant, I am not claiming that aesthetic judgments are universal. Instead I believe that if we discuss our aesthetic judgments we can understand each other's feelings across cultural divides, even if we do not feel what the other feels. If we enter into dialogue with others, we will understand their aesthetic judgments.

In the First Introduction to *The Critique of Judgment*, Kant writes that without presupposing reflective judgment all reflection would be haphazard and blind, and we would have no reason to suspect that reflection could be in accord with nature (C3, First Introduction, §V). The purposiveness of nature is not found in any particular object, but rather only in the subject. *The Critique of Pure Reason* sets out the conditions for the possibility of knowledge of objects. *The Critique of Judgment* seeks to show how the purposiveness of nature is the key for a system of laws of nature. And it is in relation to these laws of nature that Kant believes a systematic critique of taste is possible.[26] That is to say, the purposiveness of nature is the principle that allows us to deduce the a priori conditions under which our disinterested feelings of pleasure and displeasure arise.[27]

I have discussed at some length how Kant arrived at the notion of disinterested aesthetic judgments. I have done so in part out of the conviction that understanding requires intensive study. In addition, I want to show how the meaning of purposiveness changes and that the majority of Kant's book was written without recourse to reflective judgment. It is clear that Kant was deeply committed to the universality of aesthetic judgment (among northern European educated men), but constantly searching for a way to ground this universality.

Let us take up Kant's insight that aesthetics is based on reflective and not determinative judgments. At the same time, let us abandon the notion that it is only the form and not the content that matters in aesthetic judgments. In trying to understand our own and other's aesthetic judgments, we must examine the ways that our experience relates to the objects of aesthetic contemplation. Assuming that the self is a diverse entity composed of many different crosscurrents, our "individual" aesthetic judgments are already an amalgamation of perspectives, influenced by many factors such as our race, class, gender, ethnicity, and sexual orientation. This inner multiplicity, as well as the multiplicity that we encounter in our interactions with others, is the stuff of which our aesthetic judgments are made. Instead of being a spontaneous liking or disliking tied to the form of the objects of contemplation, the reflective/constructive process could be seen as a model for the way our judgments are built out of insights gathered from a number of differing points of view. Such a gathering process implies more than the mere appreciation of other points of view. It implies that our aesthetic vision is already a plethora of diverse viewpoints. Trinh Minh-ha makes a similar point:

> [T]he natures of *I, I, you, s/he, We, they,* and *wo/man* constantly overlap. They all display a necessary ambivalence, for the line dividing *I* and *Not-I, us* and *them,* or *him* and *her* is not (cannot) always (be) as clear as we would like it to be. Despite our desperate, eternal attempt to separate, contain, and mend, categories always leak.[28]

Our inner diversity becomes the starting point from which we understand the diversity of others. Furthermore, it suggests that our aesthetic judgments may be constantly modified by our experiences. They are built out of particulars that are searching for a more general explanation. Clearly, this is not what Kant had in mind when he argued that our aesthetic judgments are reflective. But Kant opens the door for such appropriations by claiming that aesthetic judgments begin with particulars and build toward the universal.

ACKNOWLEDGING INTEREST

The Critique of Judgment argues that a universal, subjective, disinterested feeling lies at the base of aesthetic judgments. Kant believes that judgments about the beautiful arise freely in the subject and that they are not the result of private or merely individual feelings.[29] The feeling of liking (*Wohlgefallen*) that accompanies the perception of something beautiful is without interest (C3,

§2).³⁰ According to Kant, when considering whether something is beautiful, we do not want to know if the existence of the thing means something to us (*irgend jemand an der Existenz der Sache irgend etwas gelegen sei*) (Ibid.). A judgment of beauty is concerned with how we feel about something in a mere observation (*Betrachtung*) of either intuition (*Anschauung*) or reflection. He uses the example of a palace to illustrate this point. The question of whether a palace is beautiful should not take into consideration the sweat of those who made it. To judge whether something is beautiful, all we want to know is if the mere representation (*Vorstellung*) of the object in us is accompanied by a liking. Kant reasons that we want to know what kind of feeling this representation produces in us. In making a judgment about the beauty of this thing, we do not want to know if we are somehow affected by the existence of this object. We cannot, Kant claims, in the slightest way be caught up with the existence of the thing if we want to be a judge in questions of taste.³¹

In section 5 Kant explains that the lack of interest exhibited in judgments of taste makes the liking that accompanies them free. It is free because the approval that accompanies an aesthetic judgment is compelled neither by the senses nor by reason. It is well known, he suggests, that hunger is the best cook. To those who are hungry, everything that is edible tastes good. It is only when our appetite is satisfied that our judgments of taste are reliable. Taste, Kant concludes at the end of the first moment of the "Analytic of the Beautiful," is the capacity to judge (*Beurteilungsvermögen*) an object through a feeling of pleasure without interest.

We can think of examples that help both to illustrate Kant's argument as well as to raise questions about it. Is it possible, for example, to be "objective" about a painting made by a friend? We may have difficulty judging a building to be beautiful that was constructed under a fascist regime. How would we view a plantation house if we knew that our enslaved ancestors had built it? But even in cases that are not so obvious, it is still questionable whether we are able to separate our interest from our liking. Is there anything about which we are completely disinterested? Are there disinterested feelings?³²

Kant tells us to put our Rousseau-inspired objections aside and look at a palace without thinking of the sweat of those who made it. But how many other "interests" "intrude" upon our aesthetic judgment of, for example, Versailles? These are moral concerns and not aesthetic concerns, Kant would say. What is our immediate reaction to Versailles? If I am an art historian and know something of the history of French architecture I may begin by noticing, for example, its similarities to Vaux le Vicomte, a chateau that served as a model for Versailles. If I am from another country in Europe, I may observe the similarities between Versailles and another chateau that is modeled after Versailles. If I am accustomed to ornate architecture, its ornateness may not impress me. The ornateness might very well be the first thing to strike someone who has spent all of his or her life living in a simple Cistercian monastery or abbey. It is difficult to imagine that a Western art historian, a Japanese businessman, and a worker from an Indonesian factory would all have the same immediate feeling as they stood in front of the palace. But I need not go in search of such "exotic" examples; I would not share the same immediate feeling as my siblings, my parents, my wife, or my children.

Kant might reply that my art historian, in making the link to Vaux le Vicomte, is already far beyond his or her initial feeling. A similar objection could be brought against my other examples. Kant would ask, what is a person's (that is, what is a northern European educated man's) immediate *feeling* when he gazes upon the chateau? Does it provoke an immediate feeling of liking? If it does, it is beautiful. But I do not believe that we can pare away our cultural baggage. Our feelings are always tied up with the particularities of our upbringing and our education. We cannot strip away the types of landscapes or cityscapes that we have seen each day of our lives. I do not even think that we can eliminate our professional training to get back to our "original feeling." If we are to communicate across the many borders that seem to separate us from each other, we must acknowledge our interests rather than looking for a disinterested aesthetic judgment. As Hilde Hein points out, there are excellent reasons for doubting the myth of impartiality, but there may be even better reasons to doubt that impartiality is desirable.[33] She argues that divorcing aesthetics from experience trivializes it and renders it irrelevant. Furthermore, it makes aesthetic experience "a plaything of privilege."[34] She also argues that the myth of the disinterested spectator leads us to think that aesthetic judgments are best made in environments free of encumbrances, such as museums and concert halls.

In my rush to criticize Kant's notion of disinterested aesthetic judgments, it is easy to miss that one of the principal reasons for this doctrine was to ensure the communicability of aesthetic judgments. What Kant does not appreciate, in my opinion, is our ability to communicate our interests to even those who are very different from ourselves. We often will not understand other people's aesthetic values without communicating with them, but at the same time, once we engage in dialogue it becomes possible to understand their aesthetic judgments. Hooks provides examples of the ways in which communication offers us access to the aesthetic values of others.

In a number of places, hooks writes about her relationship to space in general and about her relationship to the space inhabited by southern blacks in particular. Writing of her paternal grandfather, who was a sharecropper, hooks reports that his talk about owning land and longing to build on that land "revealed and mirrored the texture of his longings."³⁵ Hooks often heard her father and grandfather discussing the house he built on this land, but was disappointed when she first saw it. She found the small square brick house "so utterly closed and tight."³⁶ Reflecting back on this experience, she writes, "Had I understood the interconnected politics of race, gender, and class in the white-supremacist South, I would have looked upon this house with the same awe as I did my favorite house."³⁷ Her favorite house was that of her maternal grandmother. In that house she learned about the importance of beauty and how to see beauty in the world. She reports that her grandmother taught her how to look—how to notice the beauty in the world around her. Her grandmother taught her to look for beauty in colors, light, and self-made objects such as quilts.³⁸

One could argue that, according to Kant, a small, functional, well-built brick house should appear to a disinterested observer as beautiful for much the same reason that Kant claimed the canoes of New World native peoples were beautiful. Simple forms appeal to Kant. What hooks suggests, against Kant, is that her aesthetic appreciation of her paternal grandfather's house was never a merely immediate reaction. Aesthetic feelings are not the result of the disinterested interplay of our cognitive powers. When she first saw the house, she was disappointed because it did not conform to her notions of beautiful space. Later on, after growing to appreciate what it meant for a sharecropper to own land and build a house, she stood "in awe" of this house, although she does not claim that she found it beautiful. In both cases, hooks sees her aesthetic reactions as tied up with many other factors. We might, like hooks, not immediately appreciate her grandfather's brick house, but after she describes the life world in which the house is situated, our feelings toward the house may change. It is through conversation that hooks learned to appreciate her paternal grandfather's house, and it is through her writings that we who have never seen the house might learn to appreciate it as well.

I agree with Kant that beauty is a liking that can be related back to our overall structuring of the world. But our social reality is a more important factor in the determining of our aesthetic values than a basic feeling produced out of the interplay of our cognitive powers. Kant himself is, to my mind, an excellent example of the interconnection between our social reality and our aesthetic feelings. It is not at all surprising, given his own devotion to understanding reason and its limits, that he would find beauty in the "discovery" of the coherency in nature's laws. Our aesthetic judgments are inexorably bound up with our cognitive powers, but our cognitive powers are much more "politicized" than Kant ever imagined. Our cognitive powers are deeply rooted in our social realities.[39]

EMPIRICAL AESTHETICS

The Critique of Judgment is too rich a work to remain entirely within the mythical disinterested normative center. There are moments in the work where we are encouraged to reach across boundaries that separate and cause us to exoticize others. In section 41 of *The Critique of Judgment*, "On the Empirical Interest in the Beautiful"—the very same section in which the Iroquois and Caribs are exoticized and marginalized—Kant writes that in civilization our greatest pleasure comes from our ability to communicate with each other. Kant believes that beauty is a judgment grounded in an initial disinterested feeling but also claims that civilization causes us to become more interested in the communication of our feelings than in the initial feeling itself. At the "highest point of civilization," Kant argues, communicability becomes the measure of the worth of our sensations. Our sensations are valued only to the extent that they can be universally shared and communicated. Now, the pleasure that each person receives from the object is small in comparison to the pleasure that she or he receives from the ability to communicate.

Section 41 is built upon the distinction between "an empirical interest in beauty" and a "pure aesthetic judgment." In pure judgments of beauty, our pleasure comes about because the form of the object is particularly well suited to our cognitive powers. If one's pleasure (*Lust*) comes about because of the thing's actual existence, this is what Kant calls an empirical interest for the beautiful.

An empirical interest in beauty arises, according to Kant, only in society. There is in each one of us, Kant believes, a drive to live in society (*Trieb zur Gesellschaft*). Given this human drive to live with others, sociability, or the ability to get along with others (*Geselligkeit*), is required of all of us. Taste has a role to play in encouraging sociability. It is natural, according to Kant, to see taste as a means to encourage the sociability that is needed to follow our natural inclination and live in society, for taste is a capacity of judgment whereby we can share our feelings with everyone else. In short, because our feelings of beauty are universal, we can communicate them to everyone, and this ability to communicate with each other about our feelings of beauty encourages our social nature.

To illustrate his point, Kant writes that a human being (*Mensch*) living alone on a desert island would have no inclination to decorate either his hut or himself. (Since I am following Kant's argument, I do not use gender inclusive language here. Kant's use of nongender-inclusive language can serve to remind us of the limits of his "universality.") Nor would this solitary human seek out or plant flowers. Only in society does it occur to him to be not simply a human, but a refined human. With refinement comes civilization. Whether someone is refined is judged by whether he is capable of sharing his pleasure with others. In addition, he will not find satisfaction in an object unless he finds that his aesthetic pleasure is shared by everyone else and that he is able to communicate with everyone else about his feelings. A concern for universal communicability is something we expect based on an "original contract dictated by our humanity" (C3, §41).[40]

Kant offers two related, but distinguishable, reasons for the communicability of aesthetic feelings. Almost all schools of contemporary aesthetic thought rule out Kant's belief in universal aesthetic feelings. But Kant's second suggestion, in his empirical aesthetics, that a concern for communicability is to be expected by virtue of our shared humanity, is a way of thinking that I am prepared to defend. I reject Kant's claim that there are universal disinterested judgments of taste, but I do believe that communication across cultural barriers is possible, particularly when we acknowledge our interests, that is, when we acknowledge the particularity of who we are and resist the urge to exoticize the other. There is, as Kant claims in section 41, at least at times, even pleasure to be derived in talking to one another about our aesthetic judgments.

Kant's notion of humanity is limited. As I have already noted, Kant is not really arguing for the universal communicability of empirical aesthetic judgments. It is only when "civilization reaches its peak" that communication becomes the principal source of pleasure. In short, he is arguing that in northern Europe among cultivated men pleasure is directly tied to "universal communicability." I am convinced that we can talk with a much wider group.

I agree with Kant that beauty is a liking that can be related back to our overall structuring of the world. But our social reality is a more important factor in the determining of our aesthetic values than a basic feeling produced out of the interplay of our cognitive powers. To take Kant's example, why should we think that the shape of canoes inspires a liking associated with beauty more than body painting, feathers, or shells? Is not Kant taking his own devotion to a rational understanding of the world and then assuming that the delight that he feels at the sudden "discovery" of the coherency in nature's laws will be shared by all others?

In spite of the pleasure that communicability offers, Kant quickly abandons this empirical interest. Since this pleasure that we take from our ability to communicate is empirical and not a priori, Kant believes that this pleasure "provides only a very ambiguous transition from the agreeable to the good"(C3, §41). Pure taste offers a more solid ground for making this transition. Uncomfortable with grounding our mutual understanding a posteriori in our ability to communicate with one another, Kant trudges back to the notion of universal a priori feelings, all the while reminding us of those excluded from his universality.

We are less than certain today where, if anywhere, "civilization" has reached such a height, but many contemporary discourses continue to remind us of the distances between cultures. Much is written about the difficulty of understanding one another across cultural borders. We often assume, for example, that race, class, gender, and ethnicity so inform our aesthetic judgments that we will inevitably have difficulty in appreciating the judgments of those on the other sides of these borders.

But borders rarely cut as clearly and distinctly as we think they do. Certainly the cultural borders about which we most often speak—race, class, gender, ethnicity, and sexual orientation—are not as clearly delineated as our usage suggests. There are also other factors, particularly in aesthetics, that serve to separate us from each other. Art in general, and contemporary art in particular, are acquired tastes. How often do we find, for example, that our aesthetic judgments differ from the judgments of other members of our families, or our friends who may share with us a racial or ethnic identity, or class, or gender? It is important to explore our differences, but our very real differences should not become excuses for our lack of communication.

Starting from the Kantian-inspired maxim that our greatest aesthetic pleasure arises out of the communication of our aesthetic values, I want to consider some of the borders involved in contemporary aesthetic debates. My goal is to reexamine those that we imagine separate our aesthetic values from others.

Hooks writes that although art played many important roles in the rural African-American community where she grew up, there was a great deal of variety in her family's aesthetic views. She tells several stories to highlight the differing aesthetic reactions within her family. In "In Our Glory: Photography and Black Life," hooks writes about the role photography played in general in the lives of black southerners in the fifties (*Art*, 54–64). She also writes about how her reaction to a photograph of her father differed from that of two of her sisters. In the photograph her father is a young man in a white T-shirt standing next to a pool table in a pool hall. She sees the look on his face as "confident, seductive and cool." "There is such boldness, such fierce openness in the way he faces the camera. This snapshot was taken before marriage, before us, his seven children, before our presence in his life forced him to leave behind the carefree masculine identity this pose conveys" (*Art*, 54). To make a long story short, one of her sisters hates the photograph. A second sister—the one who received it from their father—treasures it. Hooks entitles this photograph "In His Glory" and covets a copy of it. My point in repeating this story is to underline that our reactions to images vary greatly even within families. And some of us who are not African-American women can have an appreciation for the constellation of emotions that led hooks and her sisters to their differing reactions to this photograph.

Similarly, hooks writes that her sisters remember their maternal grandmother's house differently. Hooks remembers the house as a place of beauty, while another sister remembers it as "an ugly place crowded with objects" (*Yearning*, 113). These essays demonstrate that aesthetic reactions vary greatly even among those to whom we would seem most closely related. Although reactions vary widely and race, class, gender, and a host of other things factor into our understanding of art, they do not predetermine aesthetic judgment. And in addition, depending on which borders we choose to emphasize, we may find ourselves on the same side as many who would seem at first glance quite different from us. As I have already said, contemporary art is an acquired taste that cuts across many boundaries. Race, class, gender, and ethnicity all contribute to our judgments about art and aesthetics, but there is a contemporary art culture that many of us share across these boundaries. White males have had the greatest access to the venues of "high culture," but there are many white males who are uninterested in it. In another essay from *Art on my Mind*, hooks writes very poignantly about Andres Serrano's use of blood imagery. Hooks finds in his work images that speak to her own experience of blood. Hooks's essay demonstrates that Serrano's portrayal of blood speaks to bell hooks, who shares neither gender nor ethnicity with Serrano.

I am not suggesting that communication across these boundaries is easy. My point is rather that we can communicate across these boundaries; although the process is often difficult, cross-cultural understanding is possible. It will require us, however, to change not only our ways of thinking but our ways of being. It will require those of us interested in theory to leave our comfort zones of theorizing and to actively investigate the art and aesthetic judgments of others. To acknowledge that race, class, and gender have very real significance is consistent with asserting that they do not exhaustively define who anyone is, nor do they constitute impenetrable barriers for cross-cultural understandings.

Cross-cultural understanding is possible, but in practice there is much more we could be doing to promote it. West, writing about the problems of understanding Horace Pippen's work, says that Pippen's art "reminds us of how far we have *not* come in creating new languages and frameworks that do justice to his work."[41] Pippen was an African-American artist who lived in the twentieth century. His work does not fit into many of the paradigms that dominate contemporary discourse on art. West suggests that the terms "high art" and "folk art" do not serve to illuminate Pippen's work. West asks whether the reception of black art can "transcend mere documentary, social pleading or exotic appeal" (*Keeping Faith*, 56). One framework to which West continually returns in his essay on Pippen is an Emersonian "affirmation of everyday experiences of ordinary people" (*Keeping Faith*, 56). West also refers to Dewey's *Art as Experience* in this essay. Although Pippen's work deals predominantly with scenes from the lives of working-class African Americans, West believes that the work's appeal should go beyond African Americans. And West thinks that Emerson, Dewey, and Pippen share concerns about class.

West asks us to resist characterizing Pippen's work as "primitivism" or "exoticism," the ways that West believes black artists are too often viewed in America. Analyzing a section on double consciousness from Du Bois's *Souls of Black Folk*, West writes, "Black artists are always suspect for not measuring up to rigorous standards or made to feel exotic in a white world that often associates blackness with bodily energy, visceral vitality and sexual vibrancy" (*Keeping Faith*, 61). West would not have us ignore race in analyzing Pippen's work, but at the same time he warns us against allowing race to obscure everything else about the paintings. West cautions those who would construct a "black aesthetic." An overemphasis on race could, for example, obscure the fact that Toni Morrison can be linked "more closely to contemporary Latin American literary treatments of the arrested agency of colonized peoples than with American feminist preoccupation with self-fulfillment and sisterhood" (*Keeping Faith*, 41). A similar point is made by Amiri Baraka in *Blues People*. He shows that the blues is a music that comes out of particular class locations. Although Baraka argues that the blues grew out of black experience, he also argues that many black people rejected the blues tradition. Similarly, the music in his own church included Bach and Handel and bore no resemblance to the music at "more traditional Negro Christian churches."[42] His church had to "import gospel groups or singers having a more traditional 'Negro church' sound" to satisfy the demands of some of the "older 'country' members."[43]

I am convinced that aesthetics today must rely on empirical investigations. Social factors such as race, class, and gender inevitably affect our aesthetic judgments, but communication across these borders is possible. We must begin by acknowledging our interests—and, where appropriate, our positions of privilege—instead of trying to pretend that we are objective. We can understand one another if, among other things, we resist our tendency to exoticize. In order not to exoticize, we need not only to explore difference with our rhetoric but to engage actively the art and aesthetic judgments of others.

Hooks reaffirms the claim that a great deal of pleasure comes through the communication of aesthetic value. Resisting our tendencies to exoticize the other, we learn to communicate with others across numerous cultural borders. We understand each other not because we are all alike but rather because the borders that divide us are never as sharply drawn nor as impenetrable as we think. Engaging in dialogue with each other, reading the works of hooks, West, Trinh Minh-ha, and many others, we learn more about both that which separates us and that which unites us. Hooks confirms that communicability of our aesthetic interests is of enormous importance. She writes for a wide audience and is clearly able to explain the beauty that she sees to many of us who are not female, not black, and who did not grow up in the rural south. She can even explain to her siblings, who have a difficult time understanding it, the beauty she saw, for example, in her grandmother's house. This is not to say that her siblings will then share her aesthetic judgments, but clearly we can have some appreciation for what others feel. Even as I reject Kant's claims to universality of disinterested feelings, I believe that it is possible to communicate with each other about our feelings and understand each other even though we often disagree. I am not rejecting Kant's claims to the universality of immediate feelings to claim that smaller communities share aesthetic values.

We can understand each other across numerous cultural divides. We can understand the aesthetic feelings of others even when we are not moved as they are. Kant's empirical aesthetics, where pleasure is said to arise primarily from the communicability of aesthetic judgments, provides a source and an inspiration for my project. Our aesthetic judgments are not as unified as Kant claims, but neither are they as individualistic as our contemporary world would often have us believe. If we are ready to listen and to acknowledge our interests, then we can understand one another's aesthetic judgments across cultural divides.

NOTES

1. I would like to thank Stephen Knadler, Arturo Lindsay, Rudolf Makkreel, Ronald Moore, and Louis A. Ruprecht Jr., as well as the anonymous readers from the *Southern Journal of Philosophy*, for their careful readings of earlier drafts of this chapter and their suggestions. An early version of this essay was read at the International Association of Philosophy and Literature in May 1997, and I also received several helpful suggestions at that time.

In almost all cases I have consulted Werner S. Pluhar's fine translation of *The Critique of Judgment* (Indianapolis, Ind.: Hackett, 1987), but I have in most cases modified the translations of the passages cited based on my own reading of the German original. Hereafter, references to *The Critique of Judgment* are abbreviated as C3 and followed by the section number.

2. For an example of this tendency to overlook the limits of Kant's "universality," see J. M. Bernstein, *The Fate of Art: Aesthetic Alienation from Kant to Derrida and Adorno* (University Park: Pennsylvania State University Press, 1992). Bernstein even goes so far as to introduce gender-inclusive language when interpreting a key section of Kant's argument. Such an attempt to make Kant's language more inclusive obscures the extent to which Kant never meant to be widely inclusive when arguing for the "universality" of beauty. See, for example, Bernstein's discussions of sections 7 and 19 on page 24.

3. In the earlier work, *Observations on the Feeling of the Beautiful and the Sublime*, there is no pretension that beauty is a universal feeling. *Observations on the Feeling of the Beautiful and Sublime*, trans. John T. Goldtwaith (Berkeley: University of California Press, 1991).

4. I am indebted to Robert Bernasconi for this insight. He was also helpful in suggesting that there is an important distinction between understanding someone's aesthetic judgment and feeling as someone feels.

5. According to John Zammito, *The Critique of Judgment* was, in part, a response to Herder's embracing of an aesthetic theory that, to Kant's mind, relied too heavily on the notion of enigmatic genius—*Schwärmerei*. The danger of relying too heavily on a theory of irrational genius surfaced in a challenge issued to Mendelssohn by Johann Casper Lavater. Lavater challenged Mendelssohn to convert from Judaism to Christianity "if he could not refute the arguments of Charles Bonnet for Christianity." Kant was disturbed, according to Zammito, by Herder's abandonment of the Enlightenment in favor of the "dangerous impulses of *Sturm und Drang* irrationalism." Whereas *Sturm und Drang* saw great art as the product of unexplainable genius, Kant believed great art was universal and accessible to all. See John Zammito, *The Genesis of Kant's Critique of Judgment* (Chicago: University of Chicago Press, 1992), 36.

6. Zammito, *Genesis of Kant's Critique*, 43.

7. See §40 of *The Critique of Judgment*.

8. One example of the multiplicity of identities that one can possess is given by Trinh Minh-ha. She writes of the "triple bind" of being a woman, a person of color, and a writer. Although she believes that the assigning of race or sex to a writer has long been used as a way to "cheapen and discredit" the achievements of nonmainstream writers, she still be-

lieves that it is important for women of color to reflect upon their relation to their "woman-color tradition." She also rejects the notion that one must choose between these conflicting identities. See her *Woman, Native, Other* (Bloomington: Indiana University Press, 1989), 6.

9. For a detailed discussion of the agreeable's relationship to desire, see Paul Guyer's *Kant and the Claims of Taste*. In his famous study of *The Critique of Judgment*, he has a long chapter devoted to the question of interest and aesthetic judgments. He believes that there are problems with the "official" definition of disinterestedness found in *The Critique of Judgment*. To make sense of Kant's argument for the disinterestedness of aesthetic judgment, Guyer finds it necessary to revise Kant's own account by bringing in a concept of interest from Kant's moral philosophy. Guyer admits that revising the concept of interest in *The Critique of Judgment* weakens some of the claims that Kant makes about the disinterestedness of aesthetic judgments. In particular, it restricts the claims that "the pleasure of aesthetic response is not connected to the existence of the object" and that aesthetic response does not produce an interest in its objects. See Paul Guyer, *Kant and the Claims of Taste* (Cambridge: Harvard University Press, 1979), 168. Nick Zangwill disagrees with Guyer. He claims that the presence of desire can be used to differentiate between the agreeable and the beautiful in most cases, but not all. He suggests that in some cases, particularly in the case of humor, the agreeable may not produce desire in us—at least not directly. Disinterestedness may be a necessary, but not sufficient, condition for a judgment of the beautiful. See Nick Zangwill, "Kant on Pleasure in the Agreeable," *Journal of Aesthetics and Art Criticism* 53 (1995): 166–76.

10. In §14 Kant claims that all pure, simple colors are beautiful.

11. "The Analytic of the Beautiful" is divided by Kant into four "moments." Each is further divided into sections.

12. There are other references to the Caribs in Kant's work. See, for example, *Anthropology from a Pragmatic Point of View*, trans. Victor Lyle Dowdell (Carbondale: Southern Illinois University Press, 1978), in which the Caribs are cited as an example of those who live "carelessly . . . [he] sells his sleeping-mat in the morning and in the evening is perplexed because he does not know where he will sleep during the night" (78).

13. Kant's disparagement of the use of feathers is brought out even more clearly in "The Critique of Teleological Judgment," where he writes of the foolishness of using feathers on clothes and dyes as makeup. See *The Critique of Judgment*, §63.

14. One of the most important works written on Kant's use of the word "purposiveness" is Giorgio Tonelli, "Von den Verschiedenen Bedeutungen des Wortes Zweckmäßigkeit in der Kritik der Urteilskraft," *Kant-Studien* 49 (1957–58): 154–66.

15. He gives us this order in "Von den Verschiedenen Bedeutungen des Wortes Zweckmäßigkeit in der Kritik der Urteilskraft," *Kant-Studien* 49 (1957–58): 154–66. This is a very carefully argued article that I highly recommend to any serious student of *The Critique of Judgment*.

Unfortunately Tonelli's argument for this order of composition remains inaccessible to many of us because it is presented in Italian in his *La formazione del testo della Kritik der Urteilskraft*. (In the German article cited above he merely assumes the order he developed in his book and then explains the progression of the concept of purposiveness.) Zammito, in *Genesis of Kant's Critique*, following Tonelli, agrees that §§1–22, 31–40 are the earliest sections and constitute the original "Critique of Taste." Even if Tonelli's justification for his ordering remains inaccessible to those of us who do not understand Italian, it remains accepted among Kant scholars that Kant's thinking on aesthetics underwent substantial changes in the course of writing *The Critique of Judgment*. For the purposes of this chapter, the most important of these changes comes about when Kant introduces the notion of reflective judgment into his discussion of purposiveness.

The third moment of the "Analytic of the Beautiful" represents Kant's first attempt (chronologically), in the writing of *The Critique of Judgment*, to describe the role that purpose (*Zwecke*) plays in judgments of taste. The mention that is made of purposiveness in the (second) Introduction to *The Critique of Judgment* represents, chronologically, Kant's last attempt to explain purposiveness.

According to Tonelli, the key evolution in Kant's thought comes in the way he regards nonaesthetic purposiveness. In the "Analytic of the Beautiful," Kant contrasts subjective with objective purposiveness. In the second Introduction to *The Critique of Judgment*, both the purposiveness that is described as a regulative principle of nature and aesthetic purposiveness are seen as subjective.

16. For an excellent discussion of §§10–17, see Zammito, *Genesis of Kant's Critique*, 89–105.

17. Ibid., 95–96.

18. For Derrida's discussion of these examples, and in particular his discussion of the example of the tulip, see *The Truth in Painting* (Chicago: University of Chicago Press, 1987), 83–100.

19. After the Introduction, reflective judgment is not discussed again until the end of the "Analytic of the Sublime" in the "General Comment on the Exposition of Aesthetic Reflective Judgments." In a footnote to §1 there is an obscure reference to "the power of judgment in its reflection," but there is no discussion there of reflective judgment.

20. Reflective judgment is also discussed in the First Introduction as well as the "Critique of Teleological Judgment." See for example, §V of the First Introduction and §69 of the "Critique of Teleological Judgment."

21. Rudolf Makkreel, *Imagination and Interpretation in Kant* (Chicago: University of Chicago Press, 1990), 63.

22. Ibid. See chapter 8 of Makkreel's work for his account of how aesthetic judgments for Kant are not foundational in the way that Kant believes determinative judgments are. This makes aesthetic judgments adaptable and subject to reevaluation.

23. This is a very sweeping statement, and there are other places as well where Kant does suggest that there are connections between aesthetic judgments and moral judgments. Jane Keller emphasizes the places where Kant argues for the separation between the two, for example §§5–6 of the "Analytic of the Beautiful." She finds important similarities between Kant's views on taste and on femininity. Kant views both femininity and taste, she argues, as means to further culture and civilization, but in Kant's view, neither can determine moral

or social experiences. See Jane Keller, "Discipline and Silence: Women and Imagination in Kant's Theory of Taste," in *Aesthetics in Feminist Perspective,* ed. Hilde Hein and Carolyn Korsmeyer (Bloomington: Indiana University Press, 1993).

Other studies have sought to draw upon other sections of *The Critique of Judgment* (for example, §59, "On Beauty as the Symbol of Morality," as well as many sections in "The Critique of Teleological Judgment") to bring out connections between Kant's aesthetics and his moral thinking. See, for example, Jeffery Wilson's unpublished dissertation, "Implications of *The Critique of Judgment* for a Kantian Philosophy of Action," Emory University, 1995.

24. In §9 of the "Analytic of the Beautiful," Kant claims that beauty is the product of an object, for which we have no interest, causing a quickening of the cognitive powers of imagination and understanding. It is only here in §9 that imagination takes on a role somewhat analogous to the role that it is given in the Introduction. Imagination is also mentioned in §21, and in the "General Comment on the First Division of the Analytic." In the "Analytic of the Sublime," imagination plays a much more prominent role. For more on this see Makkreel, *Interpretation and Imagination,* chapters 3 and 4.

25. Kant also stresses this point in §VIII of the second Introduction, where he argues that judgments of taste are universal if they are a reflection on the basic form of an object, without paying attention to the concept (C3, "Introduction," §VIII). The ground for its universality is found in the universal subjective conditions for reflective judgment, namely "the purposive agreement of an object (of either nature or art) with the relationship of the capacities of knowledge (*Erkenntnisvermögen*) among themselves that is required by all empirical knowledge" (C3, "Introduction," §VIII).

26. As Tonelli put this, in the Introduction that Kant published, beauty is characterized as subjective purposiveness and this is "grouped together with the subjective purposiveness of empirical laws" ("Von den verschiedenen Bedeutungen des Wortes Zweckmäßigkeit in der Kritik der Urteilskraft," 165). In nature, idealistic purposiveness serves as a regulative principle for the ordering of nature. Aesthetic purposiveness serves as a constitutive principle in relation to feelings of pleasure and displeasure. In other words, at this point Kant considers both idealistic and aesthetic purposiveness as formal and merely subjective.

27. Makkreel has suggested that, through reflective judgment, Kant saw the possibility of arriving at a communal sense that is more limited than universal laws. Somewhere between objective convictions and merely persuasive subjective opinions, reflective judgment makes possible what Makkreel labels "orientational judgments." These are judgments that produce a communal consensus that is more limited than universal judgments. Makkreel compares this to the distinction between scholastic and worldly philosophy. Scholastic philosophy is "purely speculative" and makes "doctrinal universally necessary claims." A cosmopolitan consensus, on the other hand, takes into account the fact that the dogmatic power of legal authorities inevitably limits the consensus that can be achieved in public debate. Rudolf Makkreel, "Dogmatic, Regulative, and Reflective Approaches to History," *Proceedings of the Eighth International Kant Congress,* Memphis 1995, vol. 1 (Milwaukee: Marquette University Press, 1995), 134.

28. Trinh T. Minh-ha, *Woman, Native, Other* (Bloomington: Indiana University Press, 1989), 94.

29. Nietzsche is one of the many who challenges Kant on the question of whether disinterested aesthetic judgments are possible. He suggests that it is only the ignorance of the philosophers regarding the contents of their own inner selves that allows them to make such a naive assertion that their aesthetic judgments are disinterested. See *On the Genealogy of Morals*, Sämtliche Werke: Kritische Studien Ausgabe Band 4 (Berlin: Deutsche Taschenbuch Verlag, 1980), Third Essay, 6.

30. The word *Wohlgefallen* is, I think, impossible to translate exactly into English. Werner S. Pulhar translates it as "liking." There are many problems with translating this word. One is that it must be distinguished from *Angenehmen*, which is often translated as "pleasurable." According to Kant, "*Das Wohlgefallen am Angenehmen ist mit Interesse verbunden*" (C3, §3). However, the *Wohlgefallen* that attaches to the pure judgment of taste is without interest (C3, §2).

31. Derrida's analysis of the frame in *The Truth in Painting* begins with his analysis of Kant's claim about disinterestedness. He writes that all philosophical discourses on art distinguish between the internal sense of the object and the circumstance of the object. This in turn "presupposes a discourse on the limit between the inside and outside of the art object, here a *discourse on the frame*." Derrida makes his point in a striking manner when he writes that pure disinterested pleasure does not depend, for Kant, on the empirical existence of the object, but presupposes not simply the neutralization of the object, not even simply the putting to death of the object, but the entombment of the object *(mise en crypte)* (*Truth in Painting*, 45).

32. Guyer argues that, against Kant's own self-understanding, "the disinterestedness of aesthetic response does not entail that beauty produces no interest in its object, or even its existence" (*Kant and the Claims of Taste*, 198). But Guyer still maintains that it is possible to distinguish between a disinterested delight in the mere contemplation of an object and the delight that one receives from use or possession of an object. I am arguing that the notion of a disinterested delight is a myth. Our relation to objects is always determined by our life experiences. Guyer argues that Kant shows in *The Critique of Practical Reason* that interest or lack of interest can never be established with certainty. It is rather through "hypothesis and conjecture about the causal connections in one's mental history." We establish interest, in other words, through empirical judgments, and these judgments are subject to error (*Kant and the Claims of Taste*, 205). I find Guyer's arguments useful in interpreting Kant, but I continue to find Kant's position unconvincing.

33. "Refining Feminist Theory: Lessons from Aesthetics," in *Aesthetics in Feminist Perspective*, ed. Hilde Hein and Carolyn Korsmeyer (Bloomington: Indiana University Press, 1993), 12.

34. Ibid.

35. bell hooks, *Art on My Mind* (New York: New Press, 1995), 148. (Hereafter referred to as *Art*.)

36. Ibid., 148.

37. Ibid.

38. For a discussion of the lessons hooks learned from her grandmother, see "An Aesthetics of Blackness: Strange and Oppositional" and "Aesthetic Inheritances: Histories Worked by Hand," in *Yearnings: Race, Gender and Cultural Politics* (Boston: South End Press, 1990), 103–22. (Hereafter referred to as *Yearning*.)

39. Although in §40 Kant argues that there is a place for shared communal feelings or "*sensus communis*," in aesthetics he believes that this community sense is based on an initial disinterested feeling. Kant begins §40 by noting that the term "common sense" (*gemeine Menchenverstand*) may be understood in two ways. It could mean simply the merely healthy, but not cultivated, understanding that almost everyone shares. The notion of "common human understanding" (*der gemeine Menschenverstand*) is colored, for Kant, by the fact that "*gemein*" (common) can mean both "widely shared" and "vulgar." This is true, according to Kant, in German as well as in many other languages. Kant notes that this leads some to question whether there is any advantage or merit in possessing *sensus communis*.

Kant, however, uses the term to refer to a process whereby one seeks that which is held in common in our aesthetic judgments without regard for charm and emotion. Kant defines *sensus communis* as "shared sense" or "capacity for judgment . . . which in its reflection considers the manner of representation of every other in thought in order to hold his or her judgment up to the entire human reason." The goal of this process is "*to avoid the illusion to consider subjective private conditions as objective.*" *Sensus communis* can be found, according to Kant, only to the extent that we consider not actual judgments, but rather others' possible judgments, and at the same time that we "place ourselves in the position of everyone else"(C3, §40). In response to those who would object that the process of arriving at the *sensus communis* seems like an artificial operation, Kant replies that this operation involves nothing more than merely abstracting charm and emotion to arrive at a general rule.

If one wants to understand that which we as a community share aesthetically, one must go back to the level of our capacities of judgment (*Beurteilungsvermögen*). Subjective private conditions (*subjectiven Privatbedingungen*) should not influence our judgments about what the community actually shares. It is all too easy, Kant warns, for this to happen. The key to avoiding this mistake is to recognize that that which is universally shared is limited to the formal characteristics (*die formalen Eigentümlichkeiten*) of our representation (*Vorstellung*).

But taste is "universal" for Kant. He even goes so far as to say that taste has more right to be called *sensus communis* than logic, for our common sense of taste is based on a feeling. Taste, Kant writes, can be defined as our ability to judge a representation on the basis of a feeling. A judgment of taste makes a claim that is universally (*allgemein*) communicable without reference to a concept.

40. Guyer believes that Kant is confused in §41. Guyer argues that although an intersubjectively valid pleasure could promote our social nature, our social nature could only provide an empirical, not a rational, argument for the validity of intersubjective aesthetic judgments (*Kant and the Claims of Taste*, 365). I suggest that Kant is very clear that the empirical grounding of aesthetics promoted in §41 is distinct from the route *The Critique of Judgment* has traveled up to this time. What I find exciting about §41 is that it makes an empirical

judgment about our sociability. Kant recognizes that this empirical approach is at odds with the rest of the work, but he has a strong, empirically grounded intuition that we take pleasure in talking with one another. Kant ultimately rejects this grounding for his aesthetics because he believes it is difficult to link aesthetics and morality if aesthetics is based on this empirical ground.

41. Cornel West, *Keeping Faith: Philosophy and Race in America* (New York: Routledge, 1993), 66. (Hereafter referred to as *Keeping Faith*.)

42. Amiri Baraka, *Blues People: Negro Music in White America* (New York: Quill, 1999) 58.

43. Ibid.

2

WHY NIETZSCHE (SOMETIMES) CAN'T SING THE BLUES; OR, DAVIS, NIETZSCHE, AND THE SOCIAL EMBEDDEDNESS OF AESTHETIC JUDGMENTS

I have argued that we can understand art and aesthetic judgments across cultural borders. Talking with each other, we can understand what others feel even if we do not always feel as they do. My optimism about our ability to understand the aesthetic judgments of others is grounded in the belief that art and aesthetic judgments are the products of social realities and that if we invest the time and effort, it is possible to understand a great deal about another person's social reality. Art has sometimes been taken to be the product of enigmatic genius and, at times, artistic production has been said to be a gift of the gods. I believe that art and aesthetic understanding are inevitably a product of their times embedded in their social reality.

Lovers left or leaving, the joys and sorrows of the road, jail, injustice, prejudice, lack of work or lack of money, the pleasures and evils of drink—these are the recurrent themes of Bessie Smith and Ma Rainey. They sing of the joys, trials, and sorrows of their lives and of the lives of people like them. Their genius is in part their ability to open up the world of black working-class people. Even if Nietzsche has little or no appreciation for the plight of people of African descent in the Americas, in so many other ways he seems like a good candidate to sing the blues.[1] His love troubles are the stuff of legend, as are the wanderings of his adult life. It is true that in many ways he lived a privileged life. He never suffered from racism, but he did suffer from numerous professional and personal rejections.[2] I will not tackle the question of whether white people, in general, can sing the blues.[3] The problem that concerns me here is rather the nature of artistic creation. The young Nietzsche claimed that artists are mere mediums for primordial forces. In his later works he flirts with an updated version of this solipsism by arguing, on occasion, that art is the product of the lonely genius, cut off from society and therefore inevitably misunderstood. At one point in his later writings, Nietzsche claims that a great artist forces himself on objects, enriching them "out of his [the artist's] own fullness." (I do not use gender inclusive language here because for Nietzsche great artists are always male.) In other places in his later work, Nietzsche argues that art is the product of the artist's biology.[4] To the extent that he believes art is the product of primordial drives, or the artist's biology, then Nietzsche cannot sing the blues.

Blues singers have a more sophisticated understanding of the relationship between art and life. They recognize that their art is embedded in their social reality. As Angela Davis writes, "the social circumstances of black people's lives produce an endless series of calamities."[5] These calamities, as well as the joys of love, food, and travel, make up an important part of the inspiration for the blues. Davis argues that the greatness of blues singers Ma Rainey, Bessie Smith, and Billie Holiday (admittedly a jazz singer, but deeply influenced by the blues) can only be understood within the context of their times: "Art never achieves greatness through transcendence of sociohistorical reality. On the contrary, even as it transcends specific circumstances and conventions, it is deeply rooted in social realities."[6] Amiri Baraka makes a similar point: "[E]ach phase of the Negro's music issued from the dictates of his social and psychological environment."[7]

At times, Nietzsche does recognize the social embeddedness of art. There are places where Nietzsche acknowledges that he is a product of time and claims that artists and artworks—even if they challenge their times—are products of their times and can only be understood as such. Nietzsche writes that both he and Wagner are decadent, but he fights against his decadence. This is the bluesy Nietzsche. This Nietzsche recognizes that one understands art not through the analysis of enigmatic primordial drives nor through a study of physiology, but rather through a detailed analysis of the artists and the times of both the artists and the interpreter. If art is the product of inspiration and inspiration comes from the gods—or for that matter from an enigmatic artistic genius—then I am not sure how any of us who have not been touched by the gods can understand very much of art. But, if, as the later Nietzsche sometimes suggests and blues singers never forget, art is deeply embedded in our social realities, then understanding of art comes only through intensive analyses of the life and times of both the creators and the observers of art.

Nietzsche is not as Eurocentric as Kant, but he remains in many ways a strange person to discuss in connection with the blues, and in particular with female blues singers. It is not just that he was born in the wrong place and the wrong time. I do not wish to gloss over his sexism, occasional anti-Semitism, class prejudices, or pervasive disparagement of democracy. Keeping all of this in view, I use Nietzsche's analyses of late-nineteenth-century art to explore how aesthetic judgments are tied to social life, even as art often challenges the social order. Aesthetic understanding is born from an investigation of social reality, but there is no easy transition from the understanding of social reality to the understanding of art and aesthetic judgments. As bell hooks writes, "there can never be one critical paradigm for the evaluation of artistic work."[8] Hooks calls for a radical aesthetic that would link art and revolutionary practice while at the same time envisioning an aesthetics of blackness that would be "strange and oppositional." For hooks, Davis, and the bluesy Nietzsche art is understood by placing it in its social context, but to paraphrase hooks, the relationship between social reality and aesthetic judgment will more often than not be strange and oppositional. Davis admires how Rainey, Smith, and Holiday are able to articulate "a new valuation of individual emotional needs and desires."[9] By comparing and contrasting Davis and Nietzsche, I demonstrate how art both challenges its time and yet can only be understood, to the extent that art can be understood, within the context of its time.[10]

Nietzsche's importance to twentieth-century moral thinking has long been recognized. It was Nietzsche who announced most forcefully and compellingly the death of God. He declared that it was naive to think that ethics could be based on rationality and instead suggested that we should investigate the genealogy of moral systems, that is, the study of how our systems of moral beliefs evolved. It was also Nietzsche who proclaimed the death of metaphysics and argued that science is only an interpretation and never an explanation of the world. Nietzsche plays a similar role for aesthetics. The later Nietzsche—the bluesy Nietzsche—announces the death of divine inspiration and Godly art. Having given up any hope of a rational aesthetics, Nietzsche substitutes an aesthetics based on an investigation of our aesthetic values. At his best Nietzsche is a kind of bluesy philosopher relentlessly analyzing the relationship between artists and the social world. By following the shift from the early to the later Nietzsche we can understand the genealogy of much of our modern understanding of art and aesthetic judgments.

Nietzsche is often much clearer about his dislikes than about that which he likes. He undermines our beliefs in metaphysics and ethics but does not erect new systems to take their place. Nietzsche writes about the importance of saying yes to life, but never fully develops this notion. Unlike Nietzsche, Davis uses the contributions of blues singers to envision greater human freedom as a criterion for measuring their artistic greatness. Like Herbert Marcuse, Davis argues that great art is not measured by its ability to transcend social reality but rather opens up new perspectives on the human condition. Art helps us envision a realm of freedom that does not yet exist. Clearly Davis and Nietzsche disagree on the purpose of art, and I am not going to argue that Davis's and Marcuse's suggestion is the only measurement for great art. Given the market's use of the term "great" to promote monetary value, I am deeply suspicious of the concept of greatness. But I would like to think that art can be something other than merely the undermining of traditional values. What is it that makes art worthwhile and valuable? Is innovation the only criterion that matters?

This chapter is divided into three sections. The first traces the changes in Nietzsche's thinking. In his first book, *The Birth of Tragedy,* Nietzsche argues that life is so terrible that one needs Apollonian illusions to survive. In his later works, Nietzsche underlines the way in which creative individuals question traditional values and create their own values.[11] As independent "free spirits," these creators of values are often despised by society. In his later work, Nietzsche admires those who stand apart from others, who refuse to accept "time-honored truths" and create their own highest values. For the later Nietzsche, artistic endeavor becomes the paradigmatic case of the effort of an individual to create his or her values in opposition to society's values. The later Nietzsche refers to himself as an artist to emphasize that he creates his own values instead of following the "herd."[12] In short, the later Nietzsche believes that it is possible to embrace life without calling upon Apollo. Given the later Nietzsche's desire to live for this world as opposed to sacrificing this life to gain reward in the next, one might think that he is a particularly good candidate to sing the blues. The blues unambiguously acknowledges the importance of the social world in the creation and understanding of art. But in the second section, I show how Nietzsche vacillates in his later thought among understanding art as the creation of solitary individuals, as the creation of an individual's biology, or as the creation of an individual acting within the social realm. To the extent that Nietzsche argues that art is the product of an individual's physiology, then even the later Nietzsche can't, I argue, sing the blues. In the third section I show that blues singers unambiguously maintain that their art grows out of an individual and the time and place in which that individual lives. Nietzsche sometimes remembers, but blues singers never forget, that art and aesthetic understanding are grounded in social life.

NIETZSCHE LEARNS TO SING OF THIS WORLD

Although it has recently been argued that much of Nietzsche's later philosophy of art is already present in *The Birth of Tragedy,* there are clear differences between this early work and the later Nietzsche's thought.[13] For the early Nietzsche great artists serve as mediums for the Apollonian and Dionysian drives. The paradigmatic sign of a great artist, for the later Nietzsche, is that he forsakes herd mentality and creates new values. In 1871, Nietzsche writes that the Apollonian and Dionysian are "artistic powers" (*Mächte*) or "artistic drives" (*Treibe*) that come out of nature without the mediation (*Vermittlung*) of human artists (BT, 2).[14] The contrast between the "subjective" and the "objective" artist fails to appreciate that true artists are dissolved from their individual wills and become a medium (*Medium*) whereby "the one true subject celebrates its dissolution into appearance" (*das eine wahrhaft seiende Subject seine Erlösung im Scheine feiert*) (BT, 5). In other words, artists do not create these drives, but rather serve as a medium or conduit for these naturally occurring forces (BT, 5). To be an artist is to be dissolved from one's own will into Apollonian *Schein*.[15]

These drives always remain in conflict with one another. The summit of their strife is Athenian tragedy: an equally Dionysian and Apollonian artwork (BT, 2).[16] The relevance of these forces is not reserved for Greek culture, although Nietzsche does claim that it is only from the Greeks that one can learn what the sudden rebirth of culture means for the inner life of a people (BT, 21).[17] But Nietzsche also writes that the further development of art, even in his own time, depends on the opposition of these two drives.[18]

Apollo and Dionysus are names borrowed from the Greek pantheon, to represent the Greek's nonconceptual intuitions about art.[19] Nietzsche gives an unconventional genealogy of these gods. Apollo, and not Zeus, is the father of the Greek pantheon because "the same drive that made itself visible in Apollo gave birth to the entire Olympic world" (BT, 3). The knowledge of these drives comes about not as the result of a logical insight but rather as a directly known intuition (*Anschauung*).[20]

In general, in *The Birth of Tragedy* Apollo represents the visual arts and Dionysus represents music, but this claim must be nuanced. The naive Apollonian artist par excellence, according to Nietzsche, is neither a sculptor nor a painter, but rather Homer. Nietzsche writes that one sees Homer's shining Apollonian optimism when he has Achilles say that a long, obscure life is preferable to a short, glorious one (BT, 3).[21] Nietzsche writes that Achilles' desire to live a long life—even if it were the life of a day laborer—shows an Apollonian optimism about the nature of life. Homer is an Apollonian artist in Nietzsche's schema because he uses beautiful illusions to cover the terror of existence. Dionysus is associated with music, but it is another poet, Archilochus—the wild, warrior-like servant of the Muses—who represents a forerunner to the Dionysian artist.[22] He is a Dionysian artist because he identifies himself with the pain and contradiction of the primal unity (BT, 5). There is also music that, according to Nietzsche, is un-Dionysian (BT, 17). The New Dithyrambic Music, of which Euripides was particularly fond, is an example of un-Dionysian music. Such music, according to Nietzsche, was a "slave to appearance" (BT, 17).

Apollo represents the "beautiful *Schein* of the dream world" (*der schöne Schein der Traumwelten*). The word "shimmering" may best capture what Nietzsche means by *Schein* here (BT, 1). Although Nietzsche calls Apollo the God of the *principium individuationis*, the Apollonian drive is not, strictly speaking, equivalent to it. Nietzsche writes that in the figure of Apollo the faith in the *principium individuationis* reaches its most sublime expression (BT, 1). "Through Apollo's gestures and regards, the entire desire for and wisdom of 'appearance' collects its beauty to speak to us" (BT, 1). The process of individuation does not necessarily produce shimmering Apollonian images, the images that are required to seduce us back to life in the face of the terrible Dionysian reality. Apollo represents the highest manifestation of the dream world. Greek wisdom is embodied in the saying that the best thing is never to have lived and the second best thing is to have a short life. The early Nietzsche believes that it is as an antidote to this profound pessimism that the beautiful illusions embodied in the Greek gods are needed to make life seem worth living.[23] "The Greeks knew and felt the terror and horror of existence (*Dasein*); to live they needed to place in front of this horror the gleaming dream world of the Olympians" (BT, 3). Nietzsche describes these gods as the roses on the thorny bushes (Ibid.). To appreciate the roses, one needs to experience the thorns.

Only when the Apollonian and Dionysian were equally present—that is to say in the tragedies of Aeschylus and Sophocles—did the great tragic culture of ancient Greece come forth for a very brief moment.[24] Or, as Nietzsche writes near the end of the book, at the summit of tragedy the two gods learn to speak each other's language (BT, 21). It will be hard, Nietzsche writes, for those who have never had the experience of both seeing and wishing to transcend all seeing to understand how these two drives can appear together (BT, 24).

Against the rationalism of much of eighteenth-century aesthetics, Nietzsche, in *The Birth of Tragedy*, maintains that great art necessarily involves *Schein*. Euripides kills tragedy by attempting to reconstruct it as a purely rational and therefore un-Dionysian art. How could the writer of *The Bacchae* be accused of not honoring Dionysus? According to Nietzsche, this play represents a feeble last concession of the old Euripides to the very force that he had attempted to uproot from his tragedies all his life. Nietzsche compares this final homage to Dionysus with Socrates' writing of poetry and playing of the flute during his last few days in prison. It is too little, too late, and in no way does it make up for their long lives of opposing Dionysus.

The crucial difference between Apollonian *Schein* and Euripidean/Socratic science, for the early Nietzsche, is that Apollonian *Schein* never seeks omnipotence. Socrates and Euripides, according to Nietzsche, strove to do away with the irrational. Nietzsche's Aeschylus, and his Sophocles—and even his Homer, to some extent—realized the superficiality of their illusions. They delighted in their illusions without ever forgetting the terror of existence that their illusions were meant to make bearable.[25]

When Nietzsche writes in the new preface that life depends on "*Schein*, art, deception, optic, necessity of perspective and error" he is not talking about Apollonian *Schein* ("Attempt at a Self-Criticism," BT, 5). Strictly speaking, Apollonian *Schein* is not necessary for life. When Euripides abandoned Dionysus, Nietzsche writes, Apollo abandoned Euripides. Socrates also lived in a world where the Apollonian was absent, as did Archilochus, according to Nietzsche. Indeed, most of the modern world lives without an appreciation of Apollonian *Schein*, according to the Nietzsche of 1871, as did most of the ancient world. Anyone who does not see the terror of existence—for example, all those who are overly optimistic about the power of science—will not know the sublime shimmering of Apollo. Apollonian *Schein* is only known in a few glittering moments of civilization. It burst through when Aeschylus and Sophocles presented their dramas, and in 1871 Nietzsche saw in Wagner the chance that it might rise again. The later Nietzsche rarely writes about Apollo. Neither Apollo nor the sense of *Schein* as shimmering that is associated with Apollo in the first edition of *The Birth of Tragedy* is mentioned in "Attempt at a Self-Criticism." Apollo recedes from the later work in part because existence is no longer seen as so terrible that its full experience requires the mediation of the dream world. The later Nietzsche believes that he can embrace Dionysus without calling upon Apollo. Dionysus is mentioned frequently, but the significance that this god has for Nietzsche also changes. Near the very end of his productive life, he interprets the Dionysian drive as the "yes-saying to life in its strangest and most difficult problems" (TI, "What I Owe to the Ancients," 5). He envisions a "psychology of the orgiastic" in which there is an overwhelming feeling of life and power and in which "pain works as a stimulus" (TI, "What I Owe to the Ancients," 5). Here Dionysus is no longer one of the fundamental forces of life, but rather Dionysus becomes the name for all those who say "yes to life." Whereas Nietzsche had once used the name "Dionysian" for those artists, like Archilochus, who serve as a conduit for a primordial force, now Nietzsche calls himself "Dionysian" because he affirms life in all of its struggles. Nietzsche writes that for him tragedy means:

> Yes-saying to life itself even in its strangest and most difficult problems; the will to life even when sacrificing one's highest types and being happy about one's own inexhaustability—this I called Dionysian, this I guessed was the bridge to the psychology of the tragic poet. Not to escape from terror and pity, not to purify oneself from a dangerous affect through a vehement discharge—as Aristotle understood tragedy—but rather beyond horror and pity to be one's self the eternal desire of becoming—a desire that includes in itself the desire to destroy. (TI, "What I Owe to the Ancients," 5)[26]

In a beautiful passage from *Twilight of the Idols* Nietzsche revels in his ability to sing of this world and all of its heartbreaks and adventures. The later Nietzsche did not feel that Dionysian existence apart from illusion was unbearable. This is the bluesy Nietzsche.

Nietzsche writes in the new preface to *The Birth of Tragedy* that the sentence, "only as an aesthetic phenomenon is life justified," recurs several times (*kehrt mehrfach wieder*) in the text. In the work from 1871, Nietzsche suggests that the artist is not really the creator of the artwork. It is rather that art is created by the primordial drives acting through the artist. Nietzsche writes that we are not the real creators of the art worlds, "but we can assume that we are already pictures and artistic projections for the true creator of the art worlds—for only as an aesthetic phenomenon is the existence and the world eternally justified" (BT, 5). In other words, for the early Nietzsche, we are aesthetically justified because we are phenomena created by the Apollonian and Dionysian forces.[27] He finds little value in the distinction between the objective and subjective artist, because to be a subjective artist is synonymous with being a bad artist. Every art first and foremost demands the conquering of the subjective, salvation from the "I," and the stilling of every individual will and desire (Ibid.). There is no art without pure contemplation devoid of all interest (Ibid.), but as I have argued in chapter 1, art is always tied up with interests. To understand art we must seek to understand both the role that interests play in the creation of art and the role interest plays in the understanding of art.

The early Nietzsche clearly cannot sing the blues because it is an art form that sings of and challenges the world out of which it comes. Rainey and Smith sing of lovers who have left or have been thrown out; they sing of jail time served and the joy of the road. They sing of the joys and challenges that face black people in general and black women in particular. The blues is an art form that sings of *this* world; in particular, it embraces the joys of sexuality. Davis notes that many blues singers saw a fundamental contradiction between the blues and Christianity. The sexual ethic that emphasized the freedom to pursue autonomously chosen sexual relationships was not compatible with Christian beliefs about sexual abstinence. Davis writes that "in contrast to the condemnatory and censuring character of Christianity, it (the blues) knows few taboos."[28] Both Rainey and Smith believed this and gave up the blues at the end of their lives and turned to Christianity.

Davis notes that in many ways emancipation brought a profound disappointment for recently freed slaves. She argues that in three respects the lives of blacks were changed. African Americans were no longer prohibited from traveling, education was now possible, and there was freedom to explore sexuality within autonomously chosen relationships. Travel and sexuality became two of the most important themes of the blues. To the extent that the church inhibited the right to explore one's sexuality, it was taking away, in Davis's view, one of the most important newly found rights of black people. Davis believes that a link exists between travel and sexuality. The freedom to travel is "frequently associated with the exercise of autonomy in their (black women's) sexual lives."[29] In "Farewell Daddy Blues," for example, Ma Rainey tells her "daddy" that she is wild about him and wants him all the time, but she does not want him if she cannot "call you mine." She sings that her bags are packed and that she is ready to go. Davis obviously admires the commitment to sing of this world. Given the later Nietzsche's criticism of the otherworldliness of Platonism and Christianity one would think that Nietzsche would embrace art that finds its meaning and indeed revels in the joys of this world, but, as we will see, even the later Nietzsche sometimes loses track of his own commitment to be of this world.

"THE BLUES COMES FROM BLACK PEOPLE"

In "Attempt at a Self Criticism" Nietzsche explains the phrase "justified as an aesthetic phenomenon" as meaning that his book "knows only an artist-meaning and a hidden meaning behind all occurrences" (BT, "Attempt at a Self-Criticism," 5). That is to say, there is no definitive objective meaning behind events. These artistic metaphors in the later Nietzsche underline the way in which creative individuals question traditional values and create their own values. As independent "free spirits," these creators of values are often despised by society. Nietzsche admires those who stand apart from others, who refuse to accept "time-honored truths" and create their own highest values. For the later Nietzsche artistic endeavor becomes the paradigmatic case of the effort of an individual to create his or her values in opposition to society's values. In short, the later Nietzsche is clearly distancing himself from *The Birth of Tragedy*'s contention that there is no such thing as a subjective artist. The later Nietzsche often refers to himself as an artist precisely to emphasize that he is offering us a "purely aesthetic world-interpretation and world justification" that no longer attempts to judge things by absolute values (BT, "Attempt at a Self-Criticism," 5).[30] "Purely aesthetic" here means roughly that there is no recourse to absolutes in the justification of the world interpretation.

The later Nietzsche calls himself an artist and allies himself with artists to stress that he no longer believes in truths that exist outside of social reality.[31] In the fifth book of *The Gay Science*—composed at about the same time as "Attempt at a Self-Criticism"—Nietzsche writes that it is impossible to know the extent to which existence is more than perspective (GS, 374). "We" are beyond the point where we can claim that there should only be one perspective. The world has become infinite, because we cannot exclude the possibility that it contains an infinite number of interpretations. Nietzsche ends this aphorism by discussing how one should react to this state of affairs. He asks rhetorically, who would want to deify, in the old way, this monstrosity of the unknown world. Rather than deify the unending perspective, Nietzsche's later philosophy uses the undermining of absolutes to prepare the way for the construction of new perspectives. The artist becomes the prototype of the creator of these perspectives.[32]

Artists, for the later Nietzsche, are all those who enrich things out of their own power (TI, "Raids of an Untimely One," 9). Like philosophers who no longer seek to uncover immutable truths, Nietzsche admires artists who "metamorphoses things until they mirror their power—until they are reflections of their perfection. This need to metamorphose into perfection is art. Even everything that he is not, becomes for him an occasion for joy in himself. In art man enjoys himself as perfection" (TI, "Raids of an Untimely One," 9). Nietzsche must, it seems to me, walk a fine line. What is the perfection of which Nietzsche writes here? In contrast to his earlier rejection of the role of individual creativity, the later Nietzsche wants to underline the importance of the individual in artistic creation. The risk is that Nietzsche will forget the extent to which art is the result of an interaction between the individual and the world. He is opposed to those who would impoverish the things of this world by fleeing into an other worldliness, but if he overemphasizes the notion of the artist as a solitary great individual he risks needlessly impoverishing his notion of art as well. As *Twilight of the Idols* demonstrates, Nietzsche does not write his philosophy of the future by ignoring the philosophers of the present and past. Both philosophic and artistic creation come about through a reworking of the past and present.

The later Nietzsche often seems intoxicated by his ability to deflate the icons of the modern age. At times, this sense of intoxication leads him, I think, to lose sight of what he has actually accomplished. He writes that the prototype of the great artist/philosopher is the architect.[33] The architect "represents (*darstellen*: this could also be translated as "presents") neither an Apollonian nor a Dionysian condition. Here is the great act of the will, the will that moves mountains, the intoxication of great will that arrives at art" (TI, "Raids of an Untimely One," 11). Here Nietzsche clearly distances himself from his earlier position that great artists are the medium through which the Apollonian and Dionysian forces express themselves. Now the architect is named as the model for the great artist, and the architect does *not* serve as the medium for either the Dionysian or the Apollonian. But is Nietzsche moving mountains? He is deflating the idols of modernity and endorsing art that is more life affirming. Unlike Descartes, who claims to have torn down the edifices of all prior philosophers, Nietzsche constantly revisits and reworks the ideas of those who have gone before him.

For Nietzsche, art is an antidote to morality, in particular to the morality that would sacrifice this life for the promise of an other worldly paradise. Art is "a great stimulus for life" (TI, "Raids of an Untimely One," 24). Nietzsche quickly adds that life often brings forth much that is ugly, hard, and questionable. But the tragic artist—that is to say, the great artist—has the courage to confront the terrible and frightening things that he (again, for Nietzsche great artists are male) uncovers. Many of Nietzsche's critiques of nineteenth-century morality and culture still ring true. Nietzsche has a sharp eye for some of the moral hypocrisy of his day. His problem is his uncertainty about what to erect in its place. Nietzsche offers us deconstructed modernity, not a new city on the hill.

Ma Rainey and Bessie Smith challenge society's pretensions and offer new perspectives by forcing us to reexamine that which we thought we understood. Like Nietzsche, Davis analyzes artistic production in its societal context, arguing that the artistic accomplishments of Rainey, Smith, and Holiday cannot be understood apart from the society in which they lived. Clearly these singers also embody something like Nietzsche's creation of value, but it is not creativity for creativity's sake. The threat they face is much more concrete than the flight into otherworldliness. Their lack of political rights deeply affected their ability to live their lives.

It took a "great act of the will" for these women to produce their art. Davis relates that Smith confronted the Ku Klux Klan in July 1927 when they tried to disrupt one of her performances.[34] Davis also notes that Rainey and Smith sing about the problem of male violence, but they fail to name or analyze the social forces responsible for this violence: "The blues accomplish what they can within the confines of their form. The political analysis must be developed elsewhere."[35] In other words, artistic creation comes out of a certain context and that context limits its possibilities. Davis notes that sexual assault is not referred to in either Rainey's or Smith's music. She argues that this is not surprising given that rape was not at this time an acknowledged problem of domestic relationships. In addition, this was the time when many middle-class black women were campaigning against the false charges of rape that were used to justify the lynching of black men. Given this context, it is not surprising that we find no reference to sexual assault in these women's songs. Clearly Rainey and Smith push the limits. The sexual freedom and the freedom to travel of which they sang were often freedoms reserved for men. Through their music "they forged and memorialized images of tough, resilient, and independent women who were afraid neither of their own vulnerability nor of defending their right to be respected as autonomous human beings."[36]

Artistic creation takes place within a context. This is true of the blues, abstract expressionism, impressionism, and rock and roll. There is very often something like Nietzsche's great act of the will, but that will plays itself out within a social realm. Patricia Hill Collins writes that the blues is a part of African-inspired communication patterns that "maintain the integrity of the individual and his or her personal voice, but do so in the context of group activity."[37] The later Nietzsche goes back and forth; sometimes he acknowledges the ways in which society limits art, and at other times he does not. Davis writes that

Blues singers, regardless of their ethnic backgrounds, recognize the historical connection between blues music and black experience. As blues man Houston Stackhouse put it, "Hardworking people, been half mistreated and done around—I believe that's where the blues come from . . . well the blues come from Black people."[38]

The blues takes its inspiration from individual as well as collective experiences of African Americans. The problem I am trying to highlight here is not that Nietzsche does not understand African-American experience, but that he sometimes fails to acknowledge the social origins of art. In particular, the later Nietzsche sometimes writes as though artistic creation is solely the act of an individual will. To the extent that the later Nietzsche sees art solely as the product of individual genius, he can't sing the blues.

In the fifth book of *The Gay Science*, Nietzsche borders on this when he stresses that artists are creative individuals who are often not conscious of what they are doing. Here Nietzsche refers to himself as an artist and asks, "Must we not admit, we artists, that we contain within ourselves an unbelievable difference? Our tastes and also our creative powers are, in a wonderful way, self sufficient and have their own rate of growth" (GS, 369). He illustrates what he means through the example of a musician. A musician can create things that will rub against the tastes of listeners. According to Nietzsche, the artist is often not even aware of the contradiction between his art and the tastes of the audience. Nietzsche adds that artists may not be able to keep pace with their own creations. In particular, very creative artists do not know their own works, just as parents often do not know their children. This was certainly true, according to Nietzsche, of Greek artists.[39] It is important to distinguish between this claim—that artists may not understand their own works—and the claim that an artist's work represents a complete rupture with its social surroundings. By claiming that his creative powers are self-sufficient Nietzsche approaches the claim that he creates in a vacuum.

At times, Nietzsche goes even further in this direction. At one point in the later work, Nietzsche claims again that artistic creation arises out of intoxication (*Rausch*), but now he claims that sexual arousal is the "oldest and most original form of intoxication," and that the most essential part of intoxication is the feeling of elevation of power (*Kraftsteigerung*) and fullness (TI, "Raids," 8). Great style is the result of power that no longer feels the need to prove itself (Ibid.). It comes out of spirits who no longer even notice that there are those who contradict them. It is out of a state of intoxication that artists force themselves on things: "raping them." Make no mistake, Nietzsche writes, idealization consists in "a monstrous bringing out of the principle characteristics" (TI, "Raids of an Untimely One," 8). The source of idealization is the individual. The individual creates by idealizing phenomena. Although the reference to intoxication is reminiscent of *The Birth of Tragedy*'s references to the Dionysian, there are important differences. In calling sexuality the oldest form of intoxication, Nietzsche is suggesting that aesthetic values are to be explained through reference to biology. This is the anti-blues Nietzsche.

The Case of Wagner underscores the separation of artistic creation from consciousness, but goes a step further. At times, this work advances a biological explanation for artistic creation and as such both is anti-blues and undermines Nietzsche's own recognition of the social embeddedness of art. In the epilogue to *The Case of Wagner* he writes that our aesthetic values are biologically determined. All aesthetics can be divided into two categories: the product of a declining life or the product of an ascending life. He then uses morality to illustrate his point. Master morality, for Nietzsche, is a sign of ascending life, and Christian morality is a sign of the declining life. The spirits who belong to master morality judge things according to their own inner spirit. They explain, beautify, and even make the world reasonable out of the fullness of their spirits. Christian morality, on the other hand, impoverishes and vilifies the things of this world. There is a great deal of discussion of decadence and some discussion of physiology in the later Nietzsche, but this quasi-physiological aesthetic is never fully developed.

But even within *The Case of Wagner* Nietzsche does not always hold to this anti-blues aesthetic. The later Nietzsche is disgusted with Bayreuth and in particular with what he saw as Wagner's attempt to court favor with the "masses." Much of *The Case of Wagner* is devoted to elucidating this criticism. In the preface to this work Nietzsche asks what a philosopher demands of himself. He answers that he demands that he overcome all that he carries around in himself (again I do not use gender inclusive language here; for Nietzsche only men can be philosophers). The philosopher's most difficult battle, Nietzsche continues, is with all that marks him as a child of his time. Nietzsche then makes an extraordinary confession: "I am just like Wagner a child of this time, that is to say a decadent, but I comprehended it [and] I fought against it" (CW, "Preface"). This is what I call the bluesy Nietzsche. This is the Nietzsche who realizes he is a child of his time, which is not to say that he cannot rebel. To use Jacqueline Scott's term, he is a strong decadent who is a part of his time and yet challenges his time.[40] This Nietzsche sings of this world, not the next.

Whereas Nietzsche once had great hopes that Wagner was a sign of the impending rejuvenation of German culture, the later Nietzsche divorces his hopes from Wagner and often writes as though philosophers and artists should draw only on themselves. Increasingly in his later writings Nietzsche portrays great thinkers and artists as lonely figures cut off from all others. The antisocial tenor of these writings is underlined by the use of metaphors such as rape and his constant scorn for socialism, democracy, and community.

Such a reliance on individualistic innovation as a sign of great art places Nietzsche squarely in the tradition of modern art and at the same time marks a decisive turn against his earlier model of the artist as the medium of two primordial forces. It also serves to mask, as I will now try to show, the role that community actually plays in the later Nietzsche's thought.

ART AND COMMUNITY

Much to the chagrin of the later Nietzsche the first edition of *The Birth of Tragedy* contains a mixing of ancient things and modern things. That is to say, in the early work Bach, Beethoven, Schopenhauer, and Wagner embody the possibility of a rebirth of German culture and Nietzsche writes extensively about the communal nature of Greek tragedy. The overriding concern of the Nietzsche of 1885 is for the life of the individual. In 1871 Nietzsche hopes that his analysis of Greek culture will help lead the way for the rebirth of German culture: The ancients will supply the model for the moderns. Looking back Nietzsche finds these youthful hopes for German culture to be one of the greatest embarrassments of this work. In "Attempt at a Self-Criticism" he reinterprets *The Birth of Tragedy* and suggests that it is primarily a book that offers artistic creation as a paradigm for a way of life for the individual. Greek tragedy is now seen as a model for how the *individual* can develop a pessimism of strength.

The later Nietzsche often writes as if nothing positive can come of our interactions with others. But Nietzsche's antisocial rhetoric obscures the important role that others play in the later Nietzsche's thought. As Nietzsche abandoned the notion that the artist is a medium for the Apollonian and Dionysian drives, he relied, even though he did not always acknowledge it, on the theater of social life to serve as the source for artistic and philosophic creations. The early and the later Nietzsche believe that art and philosophy should be a means to the enhancement of life, but the later Nietzsche is clearly thinking more about the enhancement of an individual's life. The later Nietzsche became more optimistic about some individuals' ability to confront life but considerably less optimistic about Germanic culture. Nietzsche's elitism is evident in both the original work and "An Attempt at Self-Criticism."[41] There is, however, a hope for the German intellectual community of his day in the original work that is completely absent from the later preface.[42] At times it would seem that there is no positive role for a community to play in the later Nietzsche's thought. However, at odds with his extreme statements about community are other texts in which Nietzsche identifies himself as a member of a community of European artists and thinkers. Art and philosophic thought come to be judged by their ability to transcend narrow national boundaries.

Both the early and the later Nietzsche denigrated politics. In *The Birth of Tragedy* Nietzsche writes of the political consequences for those cultures where the Dionysian breaks out. It is always the case, according to Nietzsche, that the first result of an outbreak of the Dionysian is an indifference to or even an opposition to one's political instincts (BT, 21). The only way that the Greeks were able to resist slipping into a total indifference toward political matters is that they combine the Dionysian and the Apollonian (Ibid.). For the short period of the tragic age they achieved a combination of Dionysian and Apollonian instincts that prevented them from falling prey to either the ascetic brooding that Nietzsche identifies with Buddhism or the imperial ambitions that he says reached their greatest, but also their most terrifying, heights in Rome. Moreover, in the original "Preface to Richard Wagner" from 1871 Nietzsche specifically warns against confusing his writing about German culture with German politics. It would be a mistake, Nietzsche writes, if his work caused its readers to reflect on the opposition between patriotic excitement and aesthetic enthusiasm (*Schwelgerei*). The hopes that Nietzsche has for a rebirth of German culture in *The Birth of Tragedy* are clearly not related to the German state.

Although he holds out hopes for the rebirth of German culture, some of the most memorable images from *The Birth of Tragedy* come from Nietzsche's biting sarcasm about the state of modern man. "Our entire modern world is caught in the nets of Alexandrian culture" (BT, 18). Modern men run up and down the banks of existence, for they no longer trust themselves to the terrible icy currents. One remains eternally hungry, a critic, or "the Alexandrian man who is finally a librarian and corrector of proofs, and wretchedly goes blind from the dust of books and from correcting printing errors" (Ibid.). Nietzsche also decries the state of art criticism in his time. When the critic becomes the master in the theater, the journalist becomes master in the schools, and the newspapers become master in society, art degenerates to a topic of conversation of the lowest kind. Such a society relies on aesthetic criticism to establish a vain, distracted, selfish, poor, and unoriginal sociability (*Geselligkeit*) (BT, 22).

Kant and Schopenhauer are distinguished from these Alexandrian men.

They possess an immense bravery and wisdom and have won the most difficult battle over optimism lodged in the essence of reason. They have pointed out that space, time, and causality belong only to the world of appearance. Some thinkers appropriate Kant and Schopenhauer to their own ends. They proclaim that the world of representation is the highest reality, with the result that—as Schopenhauer says—the dreamer sleeps even more soundly. Nietzsche compares Schopenhauer to the knight in a Dürer painting. He surveys a wasted landscape that seems totally without hope. But this landscape can change suddenly when Dionysian forces break out. What appeared dead now lives, for "tragedy always is in the middle of this abundance of life, suffering and desire, in sublime ecstasy it hears a distant melancholy song—that tells of the mothers of being whose names are delusion, will and pain" (BT, 20).[43] Kant and Schopenhauer herald the beginning of a tragic age in which at least a few see the difference between wisdom and science and value wisdom more than science. These people take on the eternal suffering of the world as their own suffering. Nietzsche asks us to think of a forthcoming generation capable of staring into the abyss, turning their back on optimism. It should not be surprising that such people would require a new art, an art of the metaphysical *Trostes* (consolation).

Surprisingly Nietzsche writes that the art in which they will find tragic inspiration is not opera but the music of Bach, Beethoven, and Wagner. These artists are capable of sparking a rebirth of German culture only because their music embodies real Dionysian force that has nothing to do with Socratic culture. In his criticism of opera, Nietzsche excludes Wagner. As such he is following Wagner, who preferred to think of his own works as "dramas." Opera, according to Nietzsche, is closely allied with Socratic culture. Wagner's "dramas" are not.[44]

Once Nietzsche moves away from the notion that the artist is a medium for primordial forces it is not surprising that he turns to the theater of human culture to find both the sources for artistic inspiration and the criteria for evaluating art. If the old eternal truths have lost most of their credence, or at least their omnipotence, where can one find the source for philosophic writing or artistic creation, if not human culture? Even as he seems to glorify the lonely thinker and artist, Nietzsche's reliance on the cultural icons of his day, as well as figures of the past, becomes increasingly evident. His philosophic creations come through reexamination and reevaluation of concepts, values, and personalities in artistic and philosophic traditions. Nietzsche now judges artists according to their relationships with their times, as well as with the past and the future. They are no longer evaluated according to their relationship to primordial drives.[45]

Although the later Nietzsche seems to have little appreciation for the positive role that community can play, there is praise for the "good European" in both *Beyond Good and Evil* and *The Gay Science*. In *Beyond Good and Evil* Nietzsche writes that he has become a southern European "by faith" and is now constantly on guard against northern European music. He longs for a supra-European music that does not fade away at the sight of the voluptuousness of the Mediterranean sky and sea. This would be a music that no longer knows anything of good and evil (BG, 255).[46]

In another place he writes that "we" are fortunate that Mozart's music still appeals to us. At some point we will no longer appreciate his "gentle enthusiasms and his childlike delight in curlicues and chinaisms" (BG, 245). Appreciation of Beethoven will disappear even faster. Beethoven is only "the epilogue of a transitional and style break and not, like Mozart, the epilogue to a great, many centuries old, European taste" (Ibid.). Mozart and Beethoven are greater than Schumann, in Nietzsche's estimation, because Schumann has only a limited sense of taste. Schumann, unlike Mozart and Beethoven, who are European events, is only a German event. In Schumann German music approaches its greatest danger: "to lose its voice for the European soul and descend into a mere fatherlandishness" (Ibid.). These artists are judged according to whether they have transcended their narrow nationalism and joined the community of European artists. Nietzsche no longer believes that atemporal objective criteria can be used to evaluate art. Art is judged by its ability to transcend the narrowness of a national border and fit into a larger transnational and decidedly social context.

This line of thinking leads Nietzsche to a striking reinterpretation of Wagner. Nietzsche writes that all deep men of the nineteenth century—including Goethe, Beethoven, Stendhal, Heine, and even Wagner—were preparing the way for the European of the future.[47] Wagner too is a European event. The greatness of these artists is judged according to their cosmopolitan appeal. In addition, the cultural relativity of artistic creation is discussed. It is not that Mozart or Beethoven will no longer be great, but future generations will be too far removed from them to appreciate them. In short, there is no independent standard for judging art. Our aesthetic judgments are inevitably the product of our times. Nietzsche states this belief in many other places as well. For example, in *The Case of Wagner* Nietzsche admits that both he and Wagner are products of their times. The difference between them is that Nietzsche fights against this decadence (CW, "Foreword").

Their political differences notwithstanding, both Nietzsche and Davis see art as enabling emancipation. Nietzsche praises art that transcends narrow Germanic bourgeois thinking. He embraces art that transcends the boundaries of good and evil. What separates Nietzsche from Davis—as well as hooks and West—is the importance that Davis places on the emancipatory possibilities for all people within art. She does not endorse any simple-minded utopian notion of art, but she praises Rainey, Smith, and Holiday for the ways in which they contributed to the emancipation of African Americans. Quoting Marcuse, Davis argues that art can offer us new perspectives on the human condition. Art helps us to envision a better world—a world that does not yet exist. There is good reason for many of the members of the Frankfurt School to be sympathetic to Nietzsche. Both Nietzsche and the Frankfurt School are deeply suspicious of liberalism. Both are suspicious of the status quo. Nietzsche, Davis, and Marcuse all write about the difficulty of challenging the status quo, but their goals are very different. Davis seeks liberation for the many, whereas Nietzsche is elitist to the core.

At times Nietzsche even demands a reintroduction of slavery. He explains that it is his "homelessness" that makes him a good European.[48] He and other Europeans are "homeless" for they are "children of the future." They are somewhat jealous of those who feel at home in this time, but the homeless ones cannot believe in modern realities. He claims not to be a conservative seeking to return to some idyllic past, nor is he a liberal believing in progress.[49] More striking, he is not a liberal because the ideas of equal rights, free society, and "no master and no servant" do not appeal to him, nor to the community of good Europeans: "We believe it is simply not desirable that the realm (*Reich*) of justice and harmony would be established in the world" (GS, 377). He writes that these homeless ones love danger, war, and adventure. They consider themselves to be conquerors and consider it necessary to establish a new order that will include slavery: "For to every strengthening and elevation of the prototype of man (*des Typus "Mensch"*) there belongs a new art of enslavement" (Ibid.). His notion of slavery is not tied to nationalism and racism. As he wrote this twenty years after the abolition of serfdom in Russia and the Civil War in the United States this call for the reintroduction of slavery—even if it is a new art of slavery—had to sound as brutal, shocking, untimely, and morally repugnant as it does to us today.[50] Even as we abhor his suggestion for the reintroduction of slavery, it is clear that one of the motivating factors for this outrageous suggestion is its untimeliness. Nietzsche's philosophic project is now tied to the creation of new values. These values will be formed in dialogue with other thinkers and artists, many of whom will be Nietzsche's contemporaries. They will be life affirming, at least for a select few.

It is difficult to see how Nietzsche's homeless ones would participate in civil society, not to mention a system of slavery. According to Nietzsche, they prefer to live alone on mountaintops. These homeless ones are too multifarious and mixed for the tastes of the Germans of his day. This metaphor of the ideal humans living on the tops of mountains underlines the extremely attenuated ties that the later Nietzsche's philosophy sometimes seems to envision between individuals in his ideal artistic-philosophic communities. His extreme distrust of collective actions, along with his glorification of the lonely individual, would seem to leave little place for artists or philosophers to exchange ideas or to inspire one another.[51] Yet at other points he makes it clear that even these homeless ones have connections with others. They live in society because they are good Europeans—the inheritance of thousands of years of European history. In short, Nietzsche's goal is the production of the elite, homeless, good European. Davis, on the other hand, sees in Billie Holiday's work "a symbiosis drawing from and contributing to an African-American social and musical history in which women's political agency is nurtured by, and in turn nurtures, aesthetic agency."[52] Art opens up new ways of thinking about our social reality that defy traditional modes of understanding. Davis sees in this great emancipatory possibilities. Nietzsche prizes art because it can lead to the flourishing of the great individual. Davis prizes it for its emancipatory possibilities for the many. Furthermore, for Davis, political and aesthetic agency nurture one another. Part of what makes Holiday great, for Davis, is her ability to transform Tin Pan Alley love songs that were contrived and formulaic. If she wanted to have a musical career, Holiday was forced to record such material. Davis argues that, for example, Holiday transforms "You Let Me Down" through her style of singing. The song tells of a woman who was told that she was an angel and put up on a pedestal. She was told that she would wear diamonds:

> I was even looking for a cottage
> I was measured for a wedding gown
> That's how I got cynical
> You put me on a pinnacle
> And then you let me down, let me down
> How you let me down

Through her style of singing, this becomes not merely a song about a woman who is "let down" by a man. It is also a complaint protesting the myriad ways that African Americans had been let down as well as an invitation for the listeners to reflect on how to move beyond the loss that they have experienced:

"The last phrase 'How you let me down,' seems to reach out and encompass a host of grievances, personal and political, inviting listeners to reflect on loss and on the possibilities of moving beyond that loss."[53] Nietzsche castigates the mentality that would sacrifice life in this world for the next. Davis is also concerned about the conditions of this world. She believes that art can help us to envision a realm of freedom that does not yet exist.

The later Nietzsche writes that there is no greater difference than the difference between art made in front of the eyes of witnesses and art that has forgotten the world (GS, 367). It is not entirely clear where he places his own art, but he seems in this passage to value the artists who forget the world. But in fact Nietzsche never forgets the world. In practice, if not in his rhetoric, Nietzsche's later philosophy is an extended engagement in debates with other thinkers and artists. One of the greatest changes from the early to the later Nietzsche is that he no longer claims it is others (i.e., Bach, Beethoven, Wagner, Kant, or Schopenhauer) who are at the crest of the rejuvenation of culture. Now it is Nietzsche himself (and his Zarathustra) who represents the great challenge to his time as well as the harbinger of the next stage of European culture.

Nietzsche can only challenge his time because he studies it. His writings are full of analyses of European (and some Asian) thinkers, past and present. Even as Nietzsche speaks of the solitary life of great individuals, in practice his philosophy was the result of a conversation with the leading thinkers and artists of European tradition. The later Nietzsche is more reliant on others than his extreme anticommunal rhetoric suggests. Having abandoned the notion of the artist as purveyor of the primordial drives, the later Nietzsche turns to others to find his artistic inspiration. Having given up on the search for eternal truths, his philosophy became, of necessity, based in social realities.

Nietzsche's reliance on social realities is illustrated by the titles of his later works: *Beyond Good and Evil, On the Genealogy of Morals, Twilight of the Idols, The Anti-Christ, The Case of Wagner,* and *Ecce Homo.* These titles all mention social phenomena that Nietzsche dissects. Nietzsche never was and never tried to be a Faust shut away in some ivory tower. Yet in spite of his involvement with his times his distrust of communal involvement ran so deep that the best he could envision from community life was a community of "higher individuals" who would occasionally band together to defend themselves (BG, 262). Much more common in Nietzsche are sentiments such as "common good is a self-contradiction" (BG, 43). He castigates narrow nationalism, anti-Semitism, and the widespread anti-Slavic feelings of his day, but at the same time his anti-liberalism is equally strong. The later Nietzsche not only abandoned the notion of a rebirth of German cultural; his glorification of the lonely artist signals a disparagement of most if not all communal involvement in the production of art. The turn toward quasi-physiological explanations for artistic inspiration can be understood, in part, as a failure to acknowledge the role that others play in inspiring us. At times, Nietzsche writes very clearly about the role that social forces play in the production of art. At other times in his antiliberal rush to underline his untimeliness he forgets his own conclusion that we are primarily socially constructed creatures. As such our artistic creations, like everything else about us, have their origins in our social environment.

But if Nietzsche calls us to embrace this world and not the next, then it must be through the embrace of some part of our social being that we embrace this world. Nietzsche would have to say that not only is hell made out of our relationships with others, but our yes saying to this world is an embrace of the social world—at least an embrace of certain parts of the social world—as well. And if this is the case, then could we not say that at some level Davis and Nietzsche agree, because both find that human potential comes about through the affirmation of some part of our social being?

We are unlikely to share Nietzsche's antiliberalism, but his emphasis on the creation of values remains one of the hallmarks of our age. Strip away his antiliberalism and Nietzsche seems to be remarkably contemporary. His emphasis on the creation of new values can be seen as a forerunner to the contemporary near deification of innovation in art. However, if we focus on his antiliberalism we quickly see the dangers associated with untimeliness. Nietzsche's writings on art challenge us to think about the ways in which artistic creation is always tied to a social context. A second challenge raised by Nietzsche's writings on art is to think about how it is possible to admit the value of learning from others and at the same time to be an untimely creator of values. A third challenge is to rethink why we value innovation.

Davis, on the other hand, knows why she favors innovation: Change is needed to promote the flourishing of the oppressed. Like Nietzsche, Davis looks to art to create new values, but unlike Nietzsche she seeks to promote social justice. She is well aware of the difficulty of defining justice and at the same time can illustrate her account with references to one of the great social movements of this century, the civil rights movement. This is a movement that is both a testament to how much has been done and how much there is left to do. Is it really enough to ask of art only that it be the product of a great will that forces us to reevaluate that which has come before? Nietzsche believes that it is through competition and individual struggle that humans achieve greatness. Great art is the product of the heroic individual will. Certainly, Davis incorporates struggle into her notion of great art, but it is the struggle to achieve a new understanding of human potential, even while it recognizes that this is a most elusive goal. And given that she has studied the blues, of course she is unambiguous about the fact that the stage on which this struggle is presented is the theater of social life.

NOTES

1. In what follows I refer to Nietzsche's works using the following abbreviations:

   BT: *The Birth of Tragedy out of the Spirit of Music*
   BG: *Beyond Good and Evil*
   CW: *The Case of Wagner*
   EH: *Ecce Homo*
   GM: *On the Genealogy of Morals*
   GS: *The Gay Science*
   TI: *Twilight of the Idols*

   The Birth of Tragedy, Beyond Good and Evil, The Case of Wagner, and *The Gay Science* are composed of consecutively numbered sections. Nietzsche often refers to these sections as aphorisms even if they are longer than traditional aphorisms. Therefore, when giving references to these works, after the title I cite the section or aphorism number. *Ecce Homo* and *Twilight of the Idols* are divided into chapters, then sections. When citing these works I give an abbreviated title of the chapter and then the section number. *On the Genealogy of Morals* is divided into three essays and then into sections. In references to this work I indicate with roman numerals the essay and then give the section number.

   In most cases I have referred to existing English translations. I greatly admire Walter Kaufmann's translations and Richard Polk's new translation of *Twilight of the Idols*. However, the translations are for the most part my own, based on the *Friedrich Nietzsche Sämtliche Werke Kristische Studienausgabe in 15 Bänden* (Berlin: Deutscher Taschenbuch Verlag, 1980).

2. For an excellent study of Nietzsche's conception of race, see Gerd Schank, *Rasse and Züchtung bei Nietzsche* (Berlin: Walter de Gruyter, 2000).

3. On the question of whether white people can sing the blues, see Amiri Baraka, *Blues People: Negro Music in White America* (New York: Quill, 1963). For another point of view see Joel Rudinow, "Race, Ethnicity, Expressive Authenticity: Can White People Sing the Blues?" *Journal of Aesthetics and Art Criticism* 52, no. 1 (Winter 1994): 127–37.

4. See, for example, the epilogue to *The Case of Wagner*. In *Twilight of the Idols*, "Raids of an Untimely Man," 20, Nietzsche writes that ugliness and beauty have physiological effects on us.

5. Angela Davis, *Blues Legacies and Black Feminism* (New York: Pantheon, 1998), 117.

6. Davis, *Blues Legacies*, 183.

7. Baraka, *Blues People*, 65.

8. bell hooks, *Yearning: Race, Gender, and Cultural Politics* (Boston: South End Press, 1989), 111.

9. Davis, *Blues Legacies*, 5.

10. What better guide can there be for answering questions about *The Birth of Tragedy* than the new preface, "Attempt at a Self-Criticism," published fifteen years after the original? Yet many questions inevitably accompany attempts at self-interpretation, and these questions are multiplied when fifteen years intervene between an interpreter and her or his work. Add to this the self-proclaimed changes that Nietzsche underwent and there are even more reasons to scrutinize Nietzsche's self-evaluations. These differences are strikingly highlighted by the reinterpretation that takes place in the new preface.

Most noticeably, Apollo disappears from the new preface and from most of Nietzsche's later writings. Neither Apollo nor the sense of *Schein* as shimmering that is associated with Apollo in the first edition of *The Birth of Tragedy* is mentioned in "Attempt at a Self-Criticism." Apollo recedes from the later work, in part, because existence is no longer seen as so terrible that its full experience requires the mediation of the dream world. The later Nietzsche believes that he can embrace Dionysus without calling upon Apollo.

One of the last times Apollo is mentioned in the works that Nietzsche published is in book 2 of *The Gay Science*. In *Twilight of the Idols* Nietzsche refers to the Apollonian and Dionysian drives, but he makes it clear that now his definition of the great artist does not necessarily involve either of these drives (TI, "Raids of an Untimely One," 11).

Nietzsche's twice-repeated claim from *The Birth of Tragedy* that his work portrays art as the highest duty and real metaphysical activity of human life—first stated in "The Preface for Richard Wagner" and then repeated in the new preface that he wrote more than fifteen years later, "Attempt at a Self-Criticism"—holds true for both the early and the late Nietzsche. But the meaning of this statement changes. Art as "the highest duty and real metaphysical activity of life" means, for the early Nietzsche, that great artists combine Apollonian illusions with Dionysian insight into the terror of existence to create great cultural moments. For the later Nietzsche, artistic creation is the real metaphysical activity because it represents the way "great individuals" create their own values.

11. Many have divided Nietzsche's work into early, middle, and late periods. See, for example, Walter Kaufmann's *Nietzsche: Philosopher, Psychologist, Anti-Christ* (Princeton, N.J.: Princeton University Press, 1974). In what follows I do not discuss what is commonly referred to as the middle work. I contrast *The Birth of Tragedy* to the works written from 1885 to 1888. For the purposes of this work, when I refer to the "early Nietzsche" I mean the Nietzsche of *The Birth of Tragedy*. By the "later Nietzsche" I mean the works written between 1885 and 1888.

12. I do not wish to suggest that he always valued artists in his later work. In *On the Genealogy of Morals* Nietzsche criticizes Wagner in particular and then artists in general for not standing against the world. Nietzsche writes that artists have been mere "valets of some morality, philosophy, or religion" (GM III, 5).

13. Julian Young argues that there is a pessimism inherited from Schopenhauer in both *The Birth of Tragedy* and the later work. See Julian Young, *Nietzsche's Philosophy of Art* (Cambridge: Cambridge University Press, 1993).

14. Several texts were written around the time of *The Birth of Tragedy* that Nietzsche himself never published. For a discussion of these texts see John Sallis, *Crossings: Nietzsche and the Space of Tragedy* (Chicago: University of Chicago Press, 1991), 7. See also M. S. Silk and J. P. Stern, *Nietzsche on Tragedy* (Cambridge: Cambridge University Press, 1981).

15. There are at least three different ways in which the words *Schein* and *Erscheinung* are used in *The Birth of Tragedy*. Two of these usages occur within a few lines of each other in "Attempt at a Self-Criticism." The Nietzsche of 1885 claims that *The Birth of Tragedy* places morality in the world of *Erscheinung*. Even in this early work morality is "placed in the world of appearance (*Erscheinung*) and not only in 'appearance' (in the sense of the idealistic technical term), but rather (morality) is classified as pretense (*Schein*), delusion, error, interpretation, contrivance, art" (BT, "Attempt at a Self-Criticism," 5). Here I translate the word *Schein* as "pretense," for Nietzsche is claiming that morality is a delusion and that even this early work recognized it as such. Moreover, Christian morality is an unnecessary illusion or a contrivance that at least some people do without.

A few lines later, while contrasting his view of art with Christianity's view of art, the word *Schein* appears again. Christianity, Nietzsche writes, is anti-artistic, for it assigns art to the realm of lies and therefore condemns it. Such an attitude is actually hostile to life, according to Nietzsche, because life depends on *Schein,* art, deception, optic, necessity of perspective and error (BT, "Attempt at a Self-Criticism," 5). Unlike the deception associated with Christianity, this time the word *Schein* is used to describe something that is necessary for life. Along with deception, perspective, and error, all human beings need *Schein* to survive.

Neither of these usages of the word *Schein* is equivalent to the shining of Apollo, as it is described in the original work.

16. Sallis claims that "there can be no doubt that tragedy surpasses the Apollonian: Apollo speaks finally the language of Dionysus. . . . Even its Apollonian images are images of Dionysus, and to this extent, it is, in the end, a double mimesis of the Dionysian" (*Crossings,* 91). What Sallis does not mention at this point is how this section of *The Birth of Tragedy* ends. Nietzsche writes that this "difficult" relationship between the two gods should be thought of as a "brotherhood." I interpret section 21 as suggesting a reciprocal relationship between the two gods rather than a predominance of Dionysus. Sallis's interpretation is colored, I think, by the importance he places on *das Maßlose* or that which is without measure.

17. This is a point upon which there is general agreement in the secondary literature. For example, Julian Young also makes this point, but goes somewhat further than I would. He claims that "Nietzsche's first thesis is not, in its most fundamental intention, a genetic thesis about Greek tragedy at all but rather an analytic and valuative thesis about great art in general" (Young, *Nietzsche's Philosophy of Art*, 31). I would only question the claim that Nietzsche's "first thesis" is a thesis about great art. It is hard to say whether Nietzsche is more concerned about Greek tragedy or great art in general. He is clearly concerned about both in *The Birth of Tragedy*.

18. Nietzsche begins the first section of *The Birth of Tragedy* with the claim that there is considerable progress to be made in the science of aesthetics.

19. When David Lenson writes that Nietzsche "feels compelled to try, however unsuccessfully, to make the alignment between his Apollo and the Greek one"(34), I think he is failing to appreciate that Nietzsche never really meant to argue that there is an exact correlation between the gods and these drives. These are names borrowed from the gods, but the drives are not co-equal to the gods. See David Lenson, *The Birth of Tragedy* (Boston: G. K. Hall, 1987).

Without mentioning Lenson, Sallis discusses this same problem. He suggests that those who critique Nietzsche for an improper use of the name of Apollo are assuming that, through the establishment of a "philologically complete inventory of the god's features," one could then determine the nature of the Apollonian (*Crossings*, 23n.). Sallis suggests, and I think he is right, that "through the figure of the god a certain understanding of art is made perceptible in that figure (Ibid.).

20. David Lenson also discusses this point. See Lenson, *Birth of Tragedy*, 24.

21. See book nine of the *Iliad*, lines 495–510.

22. Nietzsche does say that in the ancient world the lyricists and the poets were identical (BT, 5).

23. For a good discussion of the shimmering of Apollo, see Sallis, *Crossings*. The function of Apollo is a key moment in his analysis of *The Birth of Tragedy* for he, like Kaufmann, sees a decisive difference between Nietzsche and Schopenhauer. For Sallis, "Nietzsche's Apollonian is precisely the affirmation, intensification, perfection, of individuality, not its abolition" (*Crossings*, 40–41). Tragedy, for Nietzsche, does not lead to resignation from life but rather is a matter "of life's justification and transfiguration" (Ibid.). Kaufmann makes much the same point in a footnote to aphorism 7 of his translation of *The Birth of Tragedy*. See *The Basic Writings of Nietzsche* (New York: Random House, 1966), 59n3 and 60n4.

24. Actually there are times when Nietzsche sees in the dramas of Sophocles the beginnings of the end to tragedy. See Sallis, *Crossings*, on this point.

25. Sallis, in my opinion, does a very good job of elucidating Nietzsche's evaluation of Aeschylus and Euripides. I am not, however, as convinced by his reading of *The Bacchae*. See *Crossings*, 111–21.

26. My appreciation for the richness of this passage stems in large measure from my conversations with and the writings of Louis A. Ruprecht Jr. See *Tragic Posture and Tragic Vision: Against the Modern Failure of Nerve* (New York: Continuum, 1994), 137ff.

27. In the other place in which Nietzsche makes this claim in the original work (BT, 24) it is to explain how the ugliness and disharmony of the Greek myths can produce an aesthetic effect. The answer to this question, according to Nietzsche, lies in the fact that ugliness and disharmony are found in the will; that is, they are a part of the Dionysian and therefore inherent in art.

28. Davis, *Blues Legacies*, 133.

29. Ibid., 66–67.

30. In a sense, the early Nietzsche linked the artist and the philosopher, but less directly. In *The Birth of Tragedy*, citing Schopenhauer, Nietzsche writes that the philosophical man has a premonition (*Vorgefühl*) that beneath the reality in which we live there lies a second

that is covered. The Apollonian dream world where all things appear as phantoms is the sign of philosophical capability. "As the philosopher stands in relationship to the reality of *Dasein* so the artistically aroused man relates to the reality of dream" (BT, 1).

31. For example, he writes in *The Case of Wagner* that one is more of a philosopher when one is more of a musician (CW, 1).

32. In *Beyond Good and Evil*, aphorism 10, Nietzsche says that there are very few who really possess the will to truth. And those who would prefer a "certain nothing to an uncertain something" are nihilists and possess despairing, mortally weary souls.

33. Note that this is in contrast to Schopenhauer, who believes architecture to be one of the lowest forms of art. For Schopenhauer's discussion of architecture see *The World as Will and Representation*, trans. F. J. Payne, vol. 1 §43 (New York: Dover, 1969).

34. Davis, *Blues Legacies*, 37.

35. Ibid., 33.

36. Ibid., 41.

37. Patricia Hill Collins, *Black Feminist Thought*, 2d ed. (New York: Routledge, 2000), 105.

38. Davis, *Blues Legacies*, 114.

39. Nietzsche also makes this claim that great artists are usually not able to understand the significance of their own work in *Beyond Good and Evil*. Here he writes about Wagner: "Geniuses of his types Wagner seldom have the right to understand themselves" (256).

40. Jacqueline Scott, "Nietzsche and Decadence: The Revaluation of Morality," *Continental Philosophy Review* 31 (1998): 66.

41. For example, in the early work one of Nietzsche's main criticisms of Euripides is that he kills tragedy by bringing the people up on stage. The masses, according to Nietzsche, saw themselves in Euripides' plays and they were empowered to philosophize (BT, 11).

42. It is not only in the new preface to *The Birth of Tragedy* that his early hopes for German culture are criticized. In *The Gay Science* he calls *The Birth of Tragedy*'s hopes for the rejuvenation of German culture "massive errors and overestimation" (GS, 370). In *Ecce Homo* he writes that Germans can never know what music is. Bach and Handel are said to belong to an extinct German race (EH, "Why I Am So Clever," 7).

43. Kaufmann, in a note to his translation, writes of this passage that it "reads like a parody of Wagner but was certainly not meant to be satirical." *Birth of Tragedy*, in *The Basic Writings of Nietzsche* (New York: Random House, 1966), 124.

Sallis, on the other hand sees this sentence as "resuming the determination of tragedy" as well as providing "two decisive indications" about the distance involved in tragedy and the excessive nature of the Dionysian (*Crossings*, 96). Sallis argues that the distance of the song points to "the function of the Apollonian mimesis" (Ibid., 97). What these images present is not the Dionysian itself—for that remains unpresentable. "The Apollonian mimesis within tragedy produces, at a distance, images of the *Dionysian in its higher truth*" (Ibid., 98). Sallis contends that "Nietzsche does not, in the face of tragedy, become a disinterested, pure will-less subject" (Ibid., 98). This interpretation however, seems to be in conflict with the previously discussed passage from section 5 where Nietzsche claims that art demands the stilling of the will (BT, 5).

44. In *The Case of Wagner*, Nietzsche explains that Wagner preferred the word "drama" to the word "opera" (CW, 9). For a good discussion of these passages see Lenson, *Birth of Tragedy*, 90–96.

45. Adrian Piper claims that the contemporary argument that art should be apolitical has been fueled by Greenburg's formalism, a movement that gained currency under the McCarthyism of the 1950s. She suggests that there is a long-standing European tradition of seeing art as "a medium of social engagement." She sees it as particularly unfortunate for European art that it should eschew political content at the very moment when Europe's "turbulent social, political, and demographic changes offer such fertile conditions for social engagement," "The Logic of Modernism," in *Out of Order, Out of Sight*, vol. 2 (Cambridge, Mass.: MIT Press, 1996), 209–14.

46. In *The Case of Wagner* §3 Nietzsche also makes the distinction between northern and southern music and praises southern music. He even refers back to this aphorism (*Beyond Good and Evil*, aphorism 255).

47. Note that Nietzsche's estimations of people are constantly changing. In *The Case of Wagner* Nietzsche writes that it is blasphemy to group Wagner and Beethoven together. Wagner is not really a musician. Wagner's genius lay in his capabilities as an actor (CW, 8). In "Why I Am So Clever" (EC), Nietzsche repeats his claim that Wagner was a great artist and a European.

48. In *Beyond Good and Evil* Nietzsche also writes about the provincialism of those who are tied to a single nation in Europe. He writes that although the sickness of nationalism sometimes hides it, in fact "Europe wants to become one" (BG, 256).

49. In *The Anti-Christ* §4 he also disavows the notion that civilization is progressing.

50. In *Beyond Good and Evil*, aphorism 258, Nietzsche writes that a "healthy aristocracy" accepts not only slavery, but the sacrifice of a mass of people as well. In some places in the *Nachlass* he goes even further. For discussion of the issue see my *Nietzsche's Aesthetic Turn: Reading Nietzsche after Heidegger, Deleuze, and Derrida* (Albany: State University of New York Press, 1994), 153–55.

51. In *Twilight of the Idols* Nietzsche writes that, "To live alone one must be either an animal or a God—according to Aristotle. The third case is missing: one must be both—a philosopher" ("Sayings and Arrows," 3).

52. Davis, *Blues Legacies*, 164.

53. Ibid., 170.

3

MISUNDERSTANDING AESTHETIC JUDGMENTS ACROSS CULTURAL DIVIDES

My optimism about the possibility of understanding aesthetic judgments across cultural divides must be coupled with an exploration of how easy it is to misunderstand and misappropriate works of art. I turn again to an example of trying to understand across the racial divide in the United States as well as a famous debate in twentieth-century philosophy to explore the misunderstanding of art. Bell hooks charges that many critics writing on Jean-Michel Basquiat focus almost exclusively on his relationship to white mainstream artists such as Warhol. These critics, according to hooks, do not see how Basquiat's work is shaped by the suffering he felt as a person of color living in the United States. A similar charge of misinterpreting a painting has been brought against Heidegger's "The Origin of the Work of Art." Meyer Shapiro claims that Heidegger's interpretation of a Van Gogh painting of a pair of shoes reveals a great deal more about Heidegger's romanticization of the life of German peasants than it does about Van Gogh's painting. According to Shapiro, the shoes in question are not even peasant shoes, but rather shoes of a city dweller—the shoes of Van Gogh himself.

I will examine "Restitutions," Derrida's treatment of the Heidegger–Shapiro debate over the interpretation Van Gogh's painting.[1] I am looking for help in trying to determine when a work of art is being misappropriated or misunderstood. How do we decide that hooks is right, for example, about her critiques of current Basquiat scholarship, or that Heidegger is wrong to place the painted shoes on a Germanic peasant woman? I am deeply sympathetic to Heidegger's claim—seconded by Derrida—that artworks open up a world. As we will see, this understanding of the artwork helps us to understand why it is so easy to misappropriate and misinterpret art.

Shapiro's claim that Heidegger has misappropriated the shoes painted by Van Gogh seems plausible, but Derrida shows us that things are more complicated than they first seem. Derrida—or actually one of the voices in Derrida's polylogue, for Derrida's essay begins with the claim that the essay must wait "until there are more than two of us" to begin—defends Heidegger from Shapiro's attack, arguing that Shapiro fails to appreciate the role that Heidegger's attribution of the shoes to a peasant woman plays in "The Origin of the Work of Art." While criticizing Heidegger's suggestion that the shoes in the painting of Van Gogh are the shoes of a German peasant woman, one of Derrida's voices endorses Heidegger's understanding of the artwork.[2] Art does, as Heidegger suggests, open up a world, and Heidegger, Derrida, and hooks all give us clues about how we can go about understanding the artwork in the context of the world that it opens up.

Derrida recognizes that Heidegger's understanding of artworks may invite critics to project very personal agendas onto works of art. Derrida, like Heidegger, stresses our inability to decide finally on any single interpretation of art. Derrida's "Restitutions" owes a great deal to Heidegger, but it is decidedly un-Heideggerian in its breadth. Derrida and hooks open up artworks in a way that neither Heidegger nor Shapiro does because they apprentice themselves to the works about which they are writing. Occasionally Derrida's analyses stray from their subjects, but for the most part the essays of Derrida and hooks embody attentiveness to artworks and the worlds opened up by artworks. We should not presume that we can stay "at home" and obtain a rich understanding of the creative works of others. If we are to understand works of art across the numerous cultural divides that separate us, we need to follow the example of Derrida and hooks and apprentice ourselves to others. In other words, it requires considerable time and effort to understand the worlds of those who create works of art. To see one's self as an apprentice is to recognize that understanding others takes work. Apprentices have humility because they recognize that they have a great deal to learn.

Apprenticeship is a key concept for understanding other cultures. In my opinion, we can understand the art of others to the extent that we exercise the humility and diligence of an apprentice. Apprentices know that they are not the experts and have a great deal to learn. There are in art no all-knowing masters, but when we try to cross a culture border and explore a realm not well known to us then we are well advised to tread softly and to admit how much we have to learn. Humility is particularly important to the extent that one belongs to a group that has been traditionally more powerful.

I will use as an example my own efforts to understand the work of Ugandan painter Pilkington Ssengendo. His art, at first glance, may seem quite difficult for a person from the West to understand. But a closer look reveals that this art can speak to Westerners. Ssengendo was trained in the ways of Western art at the famous Makerere University in Kampala, Uganda. His work evidences Western modernist elements and African presences. It presents difficulties and challenges for both Western and African viewers. It is not readily accessible to the Bagandan ethnic group from which Ssengendo comes even though it is from the life world of this group that he has, of late, derived much of his inspiration. This book is primarily concerned with the process of understanding across the racial divide in the United States, but by considering, for a moment, the cultural divides between Ssengendo and myself we will gain some perspective on how communication across cultural divides is possible. If it is possible to understand art across continental divides, then certainly it should be possible to understand the art of those who live much closer.

One of the most enjoyable aspects of artworks is that they invite us to speculate. Artworks do open up many worlds, and we cannot finally decide about the truth in painting. But the danger here is that art's radical undecidability will lead us merely to pontificate about our own experiences. Instead of inviting us to another way of seeing, the artwork may become a venue to reify provincial notions of the world. Some explorations of art reveal merely the contours of the critic's prejudgments.

A PEDESTRIAN DEBATE

In his interpretation of Van Gogh's painting of a pair (one of Derrida's voices questions whether they are really a pair) of shoes, Heidegger appears to project his romanticized vision of a Black Forest peasant onto the work of art. Derrida believes that it is impossible to prove who owns the shoes but also argues that Heidegger is not the only one who is naive in the interpretation of Van Gogh's painting. Shapiro's attempt to prove that the shoes belong to Van Gogh himself represents a "blindness," a "putting to sleep . . . of all critical vigilance (while) lucidity remains very active, hypercritical, around this macula" (*Truth*, 279, 318). In the debate about who owns these shoes both Heidegger and Shapiro forget that they are interpreting the painting of a pair of shoes and not shoes themselves. These are not the shoes of a peasant woman, nor are they the shoes of Van Gogh. A painting should not be reduced to a mere imitation.

Derrida's voices rehearse some of the historical background of the debate. Heidegger wrote the essay "On the Origin of the Work of Art" during the 1930s when he was in the midst of his infamous involvement with National Socialism. Shapiro first read the essay on the recommendation of Kurt Goldstein, who was Jewish and fled Germany after being imprisoned there during the 1930s. Goldstein alerted Shapiro that Heidegger "hijacked" Van Gogh's shoes. The struggle over the ownership of these shoes is not, as all of this suggests, a dispassionate scholarly debate. As one of Derrida's voices eloquently points out, Heidegger's attempt to put the shoes

> on his own feet, with the pathos of the "call to the earth," of the *Feldweg* or the *Holzwege*, which, in 1935–36, was not foreign to what drove Goldstein to undertake his long march toward New York. . . . It looks as though Shapiro, not content with thanking a dead man for what he gave him to read, was offering to the memory of his colleague, fellow man and friend, nomad, émigré, city dweller,—a detached part, severed ear, but detached or severed from whom? (*Truth*, 273, 311)

In short, in the midst of their academic debate and all the appearance of civility that surrounds that debate—a civility that is a rather thin veneer for the feelings that flow between them—Shapiro sharpens his knife, cuts a piece out of Heidegger's text, and exposes some of the shoddy scholarship for which Heidegger is famous. Heidegger is wrong about this painting. The shoes in question are not the type of shoes that would be worn by a German peasant on her way home from the fields. But Derrida's voices are going to argue that although Heidegger is wrong in attributing the shoes to a German peasant, he still has a very powerful notion of the artwork.

Derrida, who is Jewish himself, recognizes Heidegger's misappropriation of Van Gogh's painting but still defends "The Origin of the Work of Art" for the power of its understanding of art. Derrida's voices argue that Shapiro is right to reproach Heidegger for being inattentive to the "internal and external context of the picture" (*Truth*, 285, 325). At the same time, Shapiro "brutally tears out the 20 odd lines" that Heidegger wrote about the peasant from the rest of the "Origin of the Art Work" (Ibid.). In other words, Shapiro is right that Heidegger has paid very little attention to the painting of Van Gogh, but

Shapiro, in turn, pays little attention to Heidegger's powerful insight about the nature of art as an opening.

It is in a discussion of the nature of the thing that Heidegger attributes the shoes to a peasant woman. There are, Heidegger argues, three pairs of determinations that have been superimposed upon the thing. The thing has been seen as (1) the bearer of its characteristics, (2) the unity of a manifold, and (3) formed matter. For aesthetics, the most important of these conceptions of the thing has been the matter/form distinction. Heidegger is in no way endorsing this understanding of the thing. He writes that "form and content are the most hackneyed concepts (*Allerweltsbegriffe*) under which anything and everything may be subsumed."[3]

Derrida's voices point out that reference is made to a pair of shoes three times before there is any mention of Van Gogh's picture. One of the voices claims that in the last of these three places "an essential schema is set in place" (*Truth*, 297, 339). Here Heidegger compares *das Zeug* and *das Schuhzeug* in particular to an artwork and to a mere thing.[4] *Das Zeug*—which Derrida translates as "product" (*produit*)—exists between the mere thing (Heidegger gives as an example a granite boulder) and the work of art. In *Being and Time*, Heidegger had already written extensively about the importance of *Zeug* to the understanding of worldliness. There he argues that phenomenology should investigate those things nearest to us. The world is littered with a plethora of ways of caring (*zerstreut in eine Mannigfaltigkeit von Weisen des Besorgens*).[5] Heidegger chooses these things—the everyday things of our world—to investigate the question of worldliness. He describes the *Zeug* as a being with which we stand in a caring relationship, and as examples of *Zeug* he gives writing instruments, sewing instruments, tools (*Werkzeug*), transportation (*Fahrzeug*), and measuring instruments. He writes that a *Zeug* in the strictest sense does not exist, but that a *Zeug* always belongs to a totality of *Zeug* (*ein Zeugganzes*) and it is within this totality that the *Zeug* can be what it is. A room is not merely the space between four walls but consists of tables, lamps, furniture, windows, and doors. Similarly, a pen is not merely a pen, for Heidegger, but belongs to a *Verweisungsmannigfaltigkeit,* a manifold of references (pen, ink, blotter, lamp, desk). In addition, a *Zeug* must be seen as that which serves a purpose, what Heidegger calls the "in order to" ("*um-zu*") nature of the *Zeug*. It is in the investigation of this manifold that we are to understand the being of the *Zeug*, but we must go about this investigation in the right way. The being of the hammer or the pen is known through it readiness to hand (*Zuhandenheit*). If we rely solely on conceptual knowledge or theoretical knowledge we are likely to miss this ready-to-hand character of *Zeug*. Heidegger writes that ready-to-hand familiarity with a *Zeug* is in itself a kind of knowledge that is far from blind.

Heidegger suggests in the "Origin of the Work of Art" that it might be easy to confuse an artwork with the making of a piece of equipment. In fact, the two processes are very far from each other. *Zeuge* are determined by their usability. The work of art, on the other hand, is determined by the fact that its createdness "is part of the created work" ("Origin," 64, 51). This is not to say, according to Heidegger, that we see the workings of the artist on the work. The artist is inconsequential to the artwork ("Origin," 40, 25). What is of consequence is that the fact "that it is" appears in the artwork. In a *Zeug* we see merely the usefulness of the *Zeug*, but in the artwork the fact *that it is* stands out. We notice a hammer's existence, but its existence soon gets lost in its useful everyday character. An artwork, on the other hand, constantly reminds us of its createdness. By refusing to be merely a *Zeug* and by constantly reminding us of its createdness, the work transports us out of the ordinary everyday experiences and transforms our relationship to the world and to the earth. It subverts our normal ways of seeing, knowing, looking, and evaluating. Heidegger never mentions the blues, but given my concerns I would illustrate Heidegger's point by saying that a blues singer can take an ordinary object—a train, a bottle, or a bed, for example—and make it stand out in a way that it opens up the world of working-class African Americans. To use Heidegger's own example, Van Gogh has taken an ordinary pair of shoes and opened up the world of a German peasant. Heidegger may be right about the general point that artworks open up worlds, but as Shapiro shows, there is good reason to question whether Heidegger has been attentive to Van Gogh's painting.

Heidegger has a suspicion, according to a Derridian voice, that we derive our notion of the thing as product (Derrida's translation of *Zeug*), in this case shoes, from our notion of simple things (in this case the granite.) What Heidegger is describing when he turns to the peasant woman is not the shoes in the painting but rather the *Zeug* of any pair of shoes. These shoes belong to a world. As *Zeug*, Heidegger suggests that the peasant woman knows these shoes primarily through care. But the question that concerns me is how we know the truth of the *Zeug* in a world that is, in some or perhaps many ways, separated from us. To use the example of the shoes, how do we know the world to which these shoes belong, if we are ignorant about Van Gogh and his world? In the worlds where we live we have many things ready to hand. We "know" these things intimately. But we often do not have this type of ready-to-hand knowledge of things outside our cultural realms. To understand the art of another culture we must rely on theory precisely because we do not have ready-to-hand knowledge.

According to Derrida's voices, the reference to the painting by Van Gogh appears at the point where Heidegger is trying "to interpret the being-product (*Zeug*) without or before the matter-form copula" (*Truth*, 300, 343). Heidegger attempts this not by subtracting the product (*Zeug*) but "by opening up *another* road toward what is properly product (*Zeug*) in the product (*Zeug*)" (Ibid.). Heidegger is compared to a cobbler who, with craftsmanlike subtlety, is going from inside the picture to the being-product (*Zeug*) that is outside the artwork. Heidegger speaks first of the picture and then of something quite different outside the picture: the life of the peasant woman. The passage describing the peasant woman's life is not primarily concerned with painting. Heidegger is a cobbler who, through a lacing movement, is passing an iron point back and forth through the surface of the canvas; "the trajectory of the reference is divided and multiplied" (*Truth*, 301, 343). In other words, Heidegger may be wrong about the painting but at the same time right about how to find the truth in painting. Truth may reveal itself in an opening as opposed to scientific understandings. To understand artworks we must become cobblers and stitch these artworks to the life worlds out of which they come. This is a never-ending process. Indeed this is, I think, a valuable way to understand art. I also have been arguing that to understand a work of art, one must understand the world out of which it comes. I too believe that art must be reattached to the world out of which it comes, but Shapiro's point, to use Derridian language, is that in lacing the painting to a pair of Germanic feet Heidegger is going very far afield from the intentions of the artist and even the nature of the shoes after which the painting seems to be modeled. Of course, the truth of a painting is not to be found only in the intentions of the artist. Furthermore, a painting may invoke many things in our minds, but it is hard to see how Heidegger, in the twenty lines that tie Van Gogh's painting to the peasant woman's feet, is doing anything other than projecting his philosophical and cultural concerns onto a canvas. The painting has served as a midwife to bring forth Heidegger's own ideas. There is little evidence that he has attempted to learn much about Van Gogh's world or the world that Van Gogh was painting.[6] Heidegger's analysis of the painting is, to use Heideggerian language, a closing of the painting rather than an opening of the painting. Heidegger's hermeneutics has hermetically sealed Van Gogh's painting. Even more important, is there something about Heidegger's way of interpreting works of art that is particularly susceptible to this?

As one voice explains near the end of Derrida's essay, Van Gogh has painted many shoes. They can be rented out, gambled for, taken, but never possessed. You can only give them back if you have possession of them (Truth, 381, 435). The truth in painting is decidedly not something that any of us possesses. Truth constantly frustrates our attempts at possession. The truth in painting must be judged according to its own very unique standards. The truth of art is not that art is a representation of something. When Shapiro criticizes Heidegger he writes as if he forgets this. Van Gogh's painting is not to be explained merely as a representation of a pair of shoes. To assert, as Shapiro does, that the shoes in question are Van Gogh's shoes is to forget, as Heidegger is trying to say, that paintings are much more than mere representations. Although there is a recognition of the danger of Heidegger's hijacking of the painting, at least one voice in Derrida's essay still sees value in Heidegger's questioning of the artwork. In particular, it stresses the importance of Heidegger's claim that in the artwork truth sets itself in work. By this Heidegger does not mean that the truth of the artwork is to be judged by the traditional criteria of truth, that is, adequation or agreement with what is. Heidegger thinks of truth as *aletheia* or as the unconcealment of what is ("Origin," 36, 21). It is the disclosing of a being or an opening up of the Being of a being. The truth of art lies in its ability to open up a world:

> What matters is a first opening of our vision to the fact that what is workly in the work, equipmental in equipment, and thingly in the thing comes close to us only when we think the Being of beings. . . . The artwork opens up in its own way the Being of beings. . . . In the artwork the truth of what has set itself to work. Art is truth setting itself to work. ("Origin," 39, 24)

How does art open up a world for us if we do not know that world firsthand?

This opening up John Sallis interprets by underlining Heidegger's references to stone in the "Origin of the Work of Art." Heidegger writes that the truth of stone is not revealed when one weighs stone. In other words, the truth of stone is not known through scientific testing. Nor would it be revealed if the stone were broken into pieces. Like earth and stone, the artwork "shows itself only when it is brought into the open as self-secluding, as closed off, as self-closed. This is what the artwork and only the artwork can do."[7] A temple's stoneness is "precisely what allows it to present—or rather, to give place to— the impenetrable depth of truth, the self-closure of the earth; it is what first lets truth in its abyssal difference happen, take place."[8] Or, as Heidegger himself writes: "The temple, in its standing there, first gives to things their look and to men their outlook on themselves" ("Origin," 43, 28). In other words, the life world comes together around the artwork; it is not that the artwork merely reflects a life world. In this sense, the artwork sets up a world. The artwork is also a setting forth of the earth. In the making of tools the material disappears; it gets lost in the tool's serviceability. In the artwork that sets up a world, however, the material is allowed to come into the open. The stone of the temple does not disappear, but the temple causes the stone "to come forth for the very first time and to come into the Open of the work's work" ("Origin," 46, 31).

TRUTH OF THE ARTWORK AS ABYSS

The measurements of science cannot give us the truth of art. The traditional aesthetic understanding of the artwork as a synthesis of matter and form will also lead us astray. We must instead think of the truth of the artwork in terms of opening up and unconcealment. But artworks subvert all of our traditional attempts at definition; the radical undecidability of art makes the truth of art abyssal (*ungeheuer*). In German *das Ungeheuer* refers to that which is monstrous. The truth of art is abyssal or monstrous because it falls outside our scientific ways of knowing. My suspicion is that although Heidegger asserts that the truth of the artwork is abyssal, he, at times, uses the radical undecidability of the work of art to further his own rather provincial view of the world. Does the "Origin of the Work of Art" open up the artwork, or has Heidegger reduced art to a hook upon which he hangs his clichéd vision of a Germanic world? Is there any essential difference between the Being that is opened and the, at times, provincial world that Heidegger inhabited? Has Van Gogh's painting been reduced to a mere cog in Heidegger's philosophical machinery? Is this not the inherent danger in Heidegger's understanding of the artwork?

Christopher Fynsk believes that at the heart of the essay lies Heidegger's "formal articulation of the relation of identity and difference in art."[9] Fynsk reads "The Origin of the Work of Art" in conjunction with Heidegger's project to rethink truth. He writes that for Heidegger in "The Origin of the Work of Art":

> Being needs the work . . . but is not reducible to the work; the work preserves, we might say, the ontological difference. But the tracing of this difference in the work is also the tracing of the self-refusal of human finitude, which, of course, belongs to the refusal of truth itself, but also seems uncannily excessive. Again Heidegger could not fully this notion of human finitude into his description of the event of truth.[10]

Fynsk's reading relies heavily on his analysis of the role of the limit in Heidegger's thought. Because a limit marks a relation, it is in some sense an opening to some other. A limit, to put it simply, implies a relationship with something else. The work has an abyssal quality about it because in its constitution it is inevitably related to something outside itself. The constitution of the work is such that it "must in some way mark the opening to something that exceeds the 'hold' of the work's formal boundaries."[11] Fynsk believes that this interpretation is in part at odds with Heidegger's essay and must be brought out of it. At the end of this chapter I turn to a discussion of apprenticeship. I argue that, particularly when we attempt to understand artworks that come out of cultures that are unfamiliar to us, we must assume the humility of an apprentice, but Fynsk underlines, as do Derrida and Heidegger, that artworks are never completely mastered.

For Fynsk, Nietzsche's *Ecce Homo* serves as an example of the abyssal artwork, even though Heidegger never recognized it as such. The parody that the book embodies suggests a "ferocious mockery of the Delphic 'know thyself.'" It exhibits that mastery of artistic passion is impossible. "The work points to an experience of difference that is not unifying or gathering."[12] In short, *Ecce Homo* is excessive, exceeding all attempts to gather it inside a definite frame. It is an autobiography that is an unrelenting challenge to the autobiographical form. With chapters like "Why I Am So Clever" or "Why I Write Such Good Books," Nietzsche is exploding the traditional autobiographical form.

These images of artworks exceeding all attempts to enclose them abound in the "Origin of the Work of Art." Heidegger writes that the world demands measure and the earth strives to keep itself closed. Heidegger describes the conflict between the two as a *Riß*, a tear or a rift. This is a tear that does not merely rip earth and world apart, it holds the two together and connects them back to their common ground. It "brings the opposition of measure and boundary into their common outline (*Umriß*)" ("Origin," 63, 49). Heidegger names this strife *Gestalt*. In the creation of a work, strife is put back into the earth while the earth must be brought out as that which discloses itself. In this process earth is not misused but rather freed to be itself. Heidegger describes the artwork as one of the places where the conflict between world and earth is brought out into the open. Earth and world struggle against one another; they oppose each other even while they need each other. Heidegger writes that the conflict between these two is intrinsic and essential ("Origin," 55, 41). Furthermore, it is only through this conflict that they enter into the conflict of clearing and concealing. Given that this conflict is abyssal there can be no final decision about the conflict between earth and world.

Both Fynsk and Sallis, like Derrida, emphasize the undecidability of artworks for Heidegger. Artworks resist our attempts to summarize them. Heidegger writes that language alone can bring artworks into the open, but art always escapes rationality's grasp. Fynsk and Sallis are right to point out the importance of the abyss to Heidegger's notion of truth in general and to his notion of the truth of the artwork in particular. But I agree with Fynsk that "The Origin of the Work of Art" does not always emphasize the abyssal nature of truth. Heidegger's understanding of truth sounds less than abyssal when he interprets Van Gogh's painting. The abyssal nature of art's truth provides yet another challenge to those interested in examining art across cultural borders. Even the art that comes out of cultures that we know well is never finally decided. How much harder is it then to understand art from another culture?[13] In short, the abyssal nature of art makes it easier to misinterpret it.

PRESERVING WORKS OF ART

Yet Heidegger gives us an important insight about how to go about understanding art. He writes that the entire essay in general and his talk of the work's createdness in particular is tending toward the taking of the next step. This step contains two moments. The first emphasizes how the work of art transports us out of the ordinary. It represents a thrust out of the ordinary and into the open. The second moment of this decisive step is the call for preservers of artworks. These are people who "follow" the "displacement" (*dieser Verrückung folgen*) that the artwork brings about. The work of art needs both creators and preservers. It cannot come into being without preservers ("Origin," 66, 53).[14] With this talk of preservers, Heidegger asserts that our encounters with artworks should displace our normal way of existing. The problem that almost all readers of the essay have is that Heidegger himself does not undergo this displacement in his own encounter with Van Gogh's painting. We could also say that those critics who try to interpret Basquiat's work without leaving their normal frame of reference would not be preservers of his work. But to the extent that we can understand art at all, I would agree with Heidegger that it requires something like what he calls preservation.

The talk of preserving pervades the last pages of the essay, although it is absent from both the epilogue and the addendum that were written later. Heidegger writes that "preserving is a sober urgency (*Inständigkeit*) within the abyss (*im Ungeheueren*) of the truth that is happening in the work" ("Origin," 67–68, 53). In other words, preservation requires us to attend—to attend soberly but urgently to the abyssal truth that is happening in the work. The knowledge that the preserver seeks does not attempt to transform the artwork, nor does it reduce the work to an experience or the creator of experiences for the observer. Instead the preservation of the work "moves the preservers into belonging with the truth that happens in the work" (Ibid.). The truth of art transforms the preserver.

Heidegger contrasts preserving with "the aestheticizing connoisseurship of the work's formal qualities" ("Origin," 68, 53). The proper way to preserve the work is prescribed by the work itself. It is not accomplished, however, by "painstaking handling of the works onto posterity" or by "scientific efforts to regain them" (Ibid). In preserving the work our accustomed ties to the world are transformed. All of our usual ways of doing, prizing (*schätzen*), knowing, and looking are transformed "in order to stay within the truth that is happening in the work" ("Origin," 66, 52). The openness of the work transports us out of the realm of the ordinary. This is how we let "the work be a work." In other words we are preservers when we allow the artwork to displace our normal way of seeing and experiencing. We are preservers when we submit ourselves to this displacement. Preservers do not take the work of art as a thing in the traditional sense of this word. They do not regard the work on their own terms, as a thing that is meant to produce a particular state of mind in the observer. The work must transform us if we are to be preservers. The work must be preserved "in the truth that happens by the work itself" ("Origin," 68, 55). Preservers belong to the work as essentially as creators do ("Origin," 71, 58). The difference between artists and preservers is that the work makes possible the creative ones (*die Schaffenden*), while out of its essence the work requires the preservers. As we will see in a moment, it is something like this that hooks is asking of those of us who are not African Americans when we look at the paintings of Basquiat. White Americans in particular could be preservers of such paintings only to the extent that these paintings transformed and displaced our normal ways of seeing. To the extent that white critics see only the relationship between white mainstream artists and Basquiat, they remain in their well-established ways of understanding.

For Heidegger, all true art is poetic ("Origin," 72, 61). By this he does not mean to limit art to what we normally think of as poetry. Art is "*the becoming and happening of truth*" ("Origin," 71, 57; emphasis in original). Truth is not derived from objects that are present and ordinary (Ibid.). It is the poetic nature of art that creates an openness in which everything is unusual. Poetry is not mere whimsy or fantasy. It is not, for Heidegger, primarily an imaginative endeavor; rather, poetry allows the open to happen. The open happens first in the middle of being. Through poetry the open brings beings to shine and ring out. Everything loses its everyday character and becomes uncanny. Language plays an essential role in this process. To understand language's role we must see that language is not only a vehicle for communication. Heidegger writes that language brings that which is "into the open for the first time." Without language—for example in the case of stones, plants, and animals—there is no "openness to what is" ("Origin," 73, 59). For Heidegger poetic language is that which allows beings to be more than mere instruments.

Artistic creation and artistic preservation are equally poetic ("Origin," 74, 60). The role of art is not to communicate the intention of the artist to the preserver. For Heidegger, the work of art does not prescribe a specific experience to the preserver. Like artists, preservers allow the open to happen. Preservers, like artists, bring beings to shine and ring out. Preservers allow artworks to disrupt their normal way of seeing, and the artist would seem, on Heidegger's reading, to serve as the occasion for the preserver's experience, but the artist's intentions would not be what the preserver is seeking to preserve.

For Heidegger, poetic creation and preservation involve the opening up of the throwness of a historical people.[15] He writes that "in the work, truth is thrown to the coming preservers that is to a historical group of men" (*einem geschichtlichen Menschentum*). The creation of poetry is no mere flight of fancy, nor is it the "self sovereign" act of a creative genius. Poetry—that is, art—makes a demand that is not arbitrary. Genuine poetry opens up or discloses that into which the human being as a historical being is already cast. For a historical people this is the earth, "their earth" (Origin, 75, 62). Art is not merely historical; it grounds history ("Origin," 77, 64). Both the creation and the preservation of art are modes of allowing truth to happen:

> The origin of the work of art, that is the origin of both the creators and the preservers, which is to say of a people's historical experience, is art. This is so because art is by nature an origin: an exemplary way in which truth comes into being (*Wahrheit seiend*), that is, becomes historical. (Origin, 78, 64)

Heidegger adds that he inquires into the nature of art because this inquiry prepares the way for the creators and preservers of art. The knowledge gained through this exploration decides the question of whether art is to be an origin or merely a routine cultural phenomenon. We would be then preservers of Bessie Smith's work to the extent that we allow her music to transform our usual ways of seeing and bring truth into being.

DERRIDA AS A PRESERVER

For Derrida there is nothing clear about Van Gogh's painting. It cannot be proved, as Shapiro claims, that the shoes in question are actually the shoes of Van Gogh. Nor is it clear, as Heidegger suggests, that they are the shoes of a peasant woman. Derrida insists that even Shapiro's seemingly scientific attribution of the shoes to Van Gogh himself is actually fraught with all kinds of political and personal motivations on the part of Shapiro.

One might think that Derrida's analysis leaves us incapable of deciding the truth in painting. As he writes in the introduction to *The Truth in Painting*, works of art can never be circumscribed or explained completely. There will always be something that does not fit into the frame that we construct for the work of art. In a sense this is true, but Derrida does guide us in thinking about the various ways that things are attached to the painting. Derrida seeks the "truth" of Van Gogh's painting in the endless contours of the debates that are conducted around it as well as in careful study of the painting itself. Even as he problematizes Heidegger's and Shapiro's attributions of the shoes he is not removing Heidegger's and Shapiro's contributions to the interpretation of this painting.

Derrida's essay reminds us that the shoes do not really belong to either Heidegger's peasant woman or Van Gogh. Most important for me, Derrida's analysis invokes a great deal of the context that surrounds the debate between Heidegger and Shapiro. He explores many of the "outside factors," such as Heidegger's and Shapiro's political and personal histories, that frame this debate.[16] At the same time he reminds us that none of these factors forms the definitive frame. Indeed Derrida is a master at showing us how rich and important the frame is to any picture as well as how incomplete any of our frames will finally be. Derrida is telling us a great deal about many of the worlds that the painting opens up, and he is much more careful than Heidegger or Shapiro about making naive assertions about the truth of the painting. Derrida's voices speak of Van Gogh's painting, but they also speak of the lives of the interpreters, of the ways in which the disagreement between Heidegger and Shapiro is not merely a dispassionate academic debate. Their dispute originates out of the life worlds of Heidegger and Shapiro. Derrida is attentive to Van Gogh, Shapiro, and Heidegger. He has apprenticed himself to each of their worlds. To borrow Heidegger's term, he has uncovered a great deal about the truth of Van Gogh's painting and the frame of the debate between Heidegger and Shapiro. Derrida's polyphonic text opens up these texts and the picture of Van Gogh.

HOOKS AND THE OPENING
OF BASQUIAT'S PAINTING

In her essay on Basquiat, hooks emphasizes the need to be "moved" by an artwork to appreciate it or to speak meaningfully about it. In particular, she claims that Basquiat's art is not easily understood: "designed as a closed door, Basquiat's work holds no warm welcome for those who approach it with a narrow Eurocentric gaze."[17] Too often hooks believes that critics approach Basquiat through white males such as Pollock, de Kooning, Rauschenberg, Twombly, and Warhol. She is not disputing that white artists had an effect on Basquiat, but she believes that the content of his work separates him from these white artists. Here hooks seems to be echoing Heidegger's claim that artworks demand that we follow their displacement. But actually hooks demands more from us. She wants us to inform ourselves about the world out of which Basquiat came. Artworks, particularly those from cultures that are not ready to hand, will not open up to us if we merely sit at home.

Hooks describes Basquiat's images as often ugly and violent. She believes his work is about the politics of dehumanization. It is both a critique of Western imperialism and a critique of black complicity and betrayal. There is first the pain that comes from colonialization: the "anguish of abandonment, estrangement, dismemberment, and death" that comes from the colonization of the black mind and body (hooks, 38). Basquiat's work also documents how complicity with the white power structures tears apart and ravishes black people. As examples of this hooks cites the paintings *Irony of a Negro Policeman* and *Quality Meats for the Public*.

Commodified, appropriated, made to "serve" the interests of white masters, the "black body as Basquiat shows it is incomplete, not fulfilled, never a full image. . . . Expressing a firsthand knowledge of the way assimilation and objectification lead to isolation, Basquiat's black male figures stand apart and alone. They are not whole people" (hooks, 38–39). In the middle of *Irony of a Negro Policeman* is a skull-like face. (I find the painting more macabre than sinister.) Hooks writes that these images are violent and represent the fear of being torn apart. They stand as a testimony to the destruction that takes place within black Americans who like Basquiat himself gain a measure of acceptance into white America. Similarly, she writes that *Jack Johnson* and *Sugar Ray Robinson* are not merely celebrations of black life. The black body in these paintings is always half formed and mutilated. This mutilation is obvious in almost all of Basquiat's work. His self-portraits often look like skeletons. Hooks believes that we will never understand Basquiat's art if we do not appreciate the horrors of black life. His work bears witness to the violent erasure of black people and their culture. She criticizes those who only see playfulness in Basquiat's work. She underlines the pain.

In linking Basquiat's work to the suffering of people of color, hooks does not wish to close down other ways of seeing it. She notes the failings she sees in traditional ways of interpreting Basquiat's work, but she does not repudiate them entirely. She seeks to look at his work from a more inclusive standpoint to see "the dynamism springing from the convergence, contact, and conflict of varied traditions" (hooks, 36). Hooks might agree with Heidegger that artworks need preservers, but she demonstrates what preserving might involve in a way that Heidegger imagined but never achieved, at least not in his description of Van Gogh's painting of the pair of shoes.

Derrida's work raises the question of how it is possible to make such claims about a work of art. Hooks's claims are more nuanced than Shapiro's or Heidegger's. She is not equating the picture with something outside of the picture. But hooks insists that our understanding of Basquiat's work will be impoverished if we fail to consider the social and economic conditions out of which it arose. Hooks, I believe, agrees with Heidegger that works of art open up worlds, but she underlines the importance of studying the world out of which the art comes. In its tone hooks's writing is very different from Derrida's. But both hooks and Derrida are attempting to understand the work of art through recourse to the wide field that surrounds the artwork. Heidegger, in a sense, prepares the way for this even if he himself never followed the path his writings opened up. He insists that artworks must be understood as something outside the matter/form distinction. *Zeuge* exist, Heidegger emphasizes, in social worlds that resist our attempts to define them in any easy manner. The truth of the artwork happens in the work, or truth sets itself to work in the artwork. Heidegger reminds us that great art opens up a world, but hooks reminds us that white critics have often failed to study the world out of which African-American artists come. To use Derrida's metaphor, like a cobbler, hooks passes a pointed instrument through Basquiat's canvases, lacing them to the pain of African Americans. In so doing she opens up the world of the suffering of African Americans as well as Basquiat's work. In the interpretation of Van Gogh's shoes, Heidegger remained at home in his own world.

Hooks parts company with Heidegger and Derrida and joins with Shapiro when she critiques those who interpret Basquiat without reference to the suffering of African Americans. To borrow Derrida's metaphor, Shapiro attacks Heidegger's lacing of the painting of Van Gogh to the life of Germanic peasants. Hooks attacks those who fail to lace Basquiat's art to the lives of African

Americans living in the United States. Derrida stresses the impossibility of ever completely defining the frame that surrounds a work of art, but Shapiro questions whether there is any link whatsoever between the painting and Heidegger's peasant woman. Hooks does not deny the connections between white artists and Basquiat, but she argues that the writings of many critics are seriously flawed by virtue of their omissions. Heidegger and, as we will see in chapter 4, Adorno, insist that paintings cannot be scientifically explained.[18] They are both working with impoverished notions of science. Science is often not nearly as dogmatic as they think. Scientists seem particularly sensitive to the tentative nature of their conclusions and often evidence the very things that I find lacking in Heidegger, namely an attentiveness to the object of investigation and a willingness to revisit their findings in the light of new evidence. Furthermore, many scientists see it as their obligation to share their interpretations with and receive validation from a wider community. To the extent that science really does all of these things, it seems to me to be, in some ways, a model for what understanding others demands. To the extent that science considers knowledge to be merely technical know-how, then Heidegger is right to see it as inimical to truth as *aletheia*.

APPRENTICESHIP

Shapiro and hooks argue that some interpretations are misguided because they do not pay attention to the artwork, but how do we know when we are being attentive to a work of art? If art is characterized by its resistance to a final interpretation, then how are we to judge whether we are being attentive to art? Elizabeth Spelman, borrowing from the work of Jean-Paul Sartre, has suggested that the notion of apprenticeship is helpful in understanding someone across a cultural divide.[19] Spelman agrees with Sartre that there is an important difference between imagining someone and actually perceiving another person. There is an infinite amount to know about anyone. The act of actually perceiving someone else requires one constantly to revise one's assessment as new observations bring new knowledge. But when I construct an image of someone by merely imagining that person and rely on this imagined notion, I do not have to revise because no new information is being received. As Spelman points out, even if we do not accept Sartre's characterization of the imagination, the distinction that he is drawing between imagination and perception points out the "strenuousness of knowing other people."[20] If we are actively trying to get to know someone, we forsake the easy way of merely imagining who that person is and must go about the more difficult task of actually perceiving the other. Relying on our imaginations, we can once and for all fix in our minds what the other is like. Or as Sartre states, when we conceive of something in thought we do not have to revisit it constantly. In our imaginations we can fix its essence. In the act of perception we must continually revise. If I rely exclusively on imagination and never make an effort to perceive something, then I do not have to apprentice myself to it. Apprenticeship is required when one is constantly perceiving and changing one's views according to the new information being received.[21]

Even if we are observing a work of art, the question becomes whether we have fixed, in our minds, the meaning of the work or whether we are receptive to new ways of understanding. Perhaps paintings, for example, do not change the way people do, but our understanding of art changes the more we find out about the world out of which the painting comes. Particularly when we try to understand art that comes out of another culture, it is important to be open to perspectives that originate in that other culture. If we do not know another culture very well it is easy for our preconceptions to hold sway. If we believe we come from a more "advanced" culture, then we are often quick to prejudge. To apprentice one's self means constantly to be on the lookout for new information that will help one to understand. Apprentices realize that they have a great deal to learn and are dedicated to learning. They know that they are not the experts.

In the United States apprenticeship is particularly important for white people. As hooks's discussion of Basquiat demonstrates, white critics sometimes fail to leave their own worlds when they try to interpret the art of African Americans. Hooks is far from the only black writer to make this kind of claim. African-American writers' works are replete with examples of whites misunderstanding blacks. Cornel West, for example, argues that blacks are often perceived as "threatening creatures who have the potential for sexual power over whites."[22] We will see in chapter 5 that Patricia Hill Collins makes similar claims. If we are going to break down the existing stereotypes, it will require us to forgo our accustomed ways of seeing. We will have to learn many things again. We will have to realize that many of our preconceptions are wrong. Part of the difficulty of understanding one another across racial lines in the United States is that we often think that we know more than we do. We are often more aware of the limits of our knowledge when dealing with more distant cultures. One of the challenges of cross-cultural understanding in the United States is to realize how much we do not know.

It is particularly important to take on the humility of an apprentice when we are trying to understand art across cultural borders. If we take seriously what Heidegger calls the abyssal nature of art, then art from another culture is doubly difficult to understand. For example, when I as a white male attempt to understand the work of Ssengendo, a contemporary artist from Uganda, I assume that I have a great deal to learn. We from the West who attempt to understand Ssengendo's art—or any other art that comes from areas that are unfamiliar to us—should go slowly. Patience and humility—two requirements of apprentices—are required by our unfamiliarity with the matter at hand. Understanding requires active seeking, but it also requires that we remember the limits of our fractured and always incomplete understanding of others. There is a long tradition of colonialists believing that they understood the "primitives" better than the "primitives" understood themselves. When trying to understand the art of others who come out of life worlds much different from ours, we should consider ourselves to be apprentices, albeit apprentices who have given up hope of finding all-knowing masters.

Ssengendo attended Makerere University in the sixties and studied under a South African artist and art historian, Ceil Todd. Ssengendo was strongly attracted to modernism, which Todd taught, and felt that although there would be African influences in his art, East African artistic traditions did not have much to offer to his painting. For more than twenty years he painted in a modernist style. Ssengendo's attitude toward his culture changed in the mid-1990s when he was confronted, at a conference in London, by artists from West Africa. They challenged him to return to his East African roots to find inspiration for his paintings. In particular, they challenged his belief that East Africa did not possess a rich artistic tradition from which he could draw inspiration.

Shortly thereafter Ssengendo experienced, for the first time in his life, the coronation of a Baganda king. At the ceremony, Ssengendo experienced barkcloth, a traditional cloth made out of tree bark, in an entirely new context. Barkcloth is primarily used in the burial of the dead. In its recent history Uganda has been ravaged by two brutal dictators, first Idi Amin and then Milton Obote, who was responsible for the murder of twice as many people as Amin (300,000 according to some estimates). Since 1986 the country has been ruled by Yoweri Museveni, a president who stood for election in 1996 and garnered 74 percent of the popular vote. He was reelected again in 2000. He has been, by many but not all accounts, an effective and democratic ruler. He is also in part responsible for allowing the coronation ceremony of the Baganda king that was so important to Ssengendo's art. Although not a member of the Baganda (Uganda's largest ethnic group), Museveni has allowed Uganda's ethnic groups to celebrate their ethnic heritages. It was Museveni who allowed the exiled king of Buganda to return.

Even while the country has made political and economic strides, it has been stalked by a new catastrophe, the AIDS epidemic. Uganda is one of the hardest-hit countries in the world. A few years ago, studies showed that, for example, among women coming to clinics for prenatal care, HIV infection rates were more than 30 percent. There is some cause for hope, however. The government has been very open about the problem. Condom advertisements are omnipresent, and the incidence of new infections has been cut in half. With the help of the United States, HIV testing is widely available. Still, coffin makers are everywhere to be seen in Uganda, as are the sellers of barkcloth. Ssengendo's experience of barkcloth was overwhelmingly negative and morbid until he experienced the coronation in 1993. During this coronation ceremony, Ssengendo for the first time saw barkcloth used for something other than the burial of the dead. It was used to transform the hillside on which the ceremony took place. This new experience of barkcloth became the basis for a turn in his painting. This is evident in the painting entitled *Barkcloth*. In this painting not only is the color the color of barkcloth, but the painting also captures the coarse texture.

The coronation ceremony provided the inspiration for a painting entitled *The Coronation*. There is much that I do not understand about this painting. Several figures, for example, have a prominence in the ceremony that is alluded to in the painting. Someone who understood the culture better might be able to identify them. But then again, maybe not. One of the interesting things about this painting, and Ssengendo's work in general, is that few have easy access to it. Few of us from the "outside" know very much about the traditions from which he derives some of his inspirations. Many of those who know of these traditions know little about the Western abstract painting that still molds his painting style. Certainly his own relationship with his tradition is not a static one. Heidegger's claim that art opens up a world is helpful here if we modify it somewhat. Let us say that art opens up many worlds. Ssengendo clearly inhabits many worlds. He is Bagandan but still learning about Kiganda culture. He is a product of Makerere, and he has been formed, in part, through conversations with other Africans and Europeans.

Another of Ssengendo's paintings illustrates the multitude of cultural traditions in his art. *The Witch* makes reference to a female figure out of Bugandan mythology. As I listened to Ssengendo recount his version of the legend I had the distinct impression that the painting represents a highly idiosyncratic reading of it. He spoke of it both in terms of the traditional legend and current revisions of the role of women in Uganda. Another of his paintings, *African Dictator,* was more accessible to me. Given that Amin is still alive, Ssengendo did not want to give it a more specific title. On the uniform there is a garish display of medals. There are masks in the background. Living through the time of dictatorship, Ssengendo spoke of the need to appear stupid. Appearing intelligent was an invitation for trouble. These masks represent, for Ssengendo, the blank faces one needed to put on to play stupid and survive.

Ssengendo's work does not fit neatly into any of the grand narratives of Western art, nor does it fit easily into many of the paradigms usually used to understand African art. Very few of us have easy access to this work. Yet many have at least some access to it. Even though I am separated from Ssengendo by racial and ethnic boundaries, we do have some things in common. We are both men, and we both teach at institutions of higher learning. We have both studied Western art. He has taught me a few things about East Africa and about his Kiganda culture. I have been fortunate enough to travel to Uganda three times and talk with Ssengendo as well as other Ugandans. We both live in the same time; how much easier is it, in many ways, for me to understand a contemporary African painter than the painting of an American who has been dead for 100 years. I, like everyone, have some experiences with death, and I start from these experiences to learn something about death in Uganda. We inevitably use our own experience as a starting point when we try to understand the experience of someone else. The key is to see how the experiences of the other differ from our own. As Sartre would say, it is incumbent on the apprentice to observe and learn rather than to rely on preconceptions.

Ssengendo's work, like all art, partakes of a variety of traditions. By virtue of its hybridity it stretches traditional critical perspectives and encourages the formation of new ones. We come to understand this art by comparing our experiences and learning about the cultural differences as well as cultural continuities. Understanding art across cultural divides requires us to dedicate ourselves to the construction of narratives that we assume from the very beginning will be partial, limited, and constantly revised as we learn more. Worlds open up only to those apprentices who are attentive and reach beyond their preconceptions. There is much that I have to learn about Ssengendo's work. I am not the master of it, but neither am I completely cut off from it.

Hence I propose that when trying to understand the art of another culture we consider ourselves to be apprentices—those who are trying to learn and who recognize how much we have to learn—but a strange sort of apprentices. We are apprentices without all-knowing masters. Certainly many people will know more than we do and in many cases they know better, but no one knows it all. There is much I have to learn, for example, about Ugandan art in general and Ssengendo's work in particular, but even though Ssengendo knows much more than I do I am not suggesting that he knows it all. At the same time he does know a great deal, and I have a great deal to learn from him. Thinking of one's self as an apprentice requires us to give up the philosophical conceit that the philosopher possesses a more complete understanding by virtue of *his* (and given that this is a prototypical male problem, I will forgo gender-inclusive language here) philosophical acumen. Apprentices know that they have a great deal to learn and that others know better than they do. In trying to understand the art of others we are left the humbling, exhausting, and yet often exhilarating task of exploring artworks about which we will always be learning.

Outside the temples of high culture or the castles of commercialism there is an important body of work that is as enormous as it is untapped. We no longer have the luxury of concentrating on the "great works," assuming that these are the only really important ones. And we don't have to go to Uganda to see underappreciated art. We can hear it in the blues bars of Memphis, we can see it in the quilts our grandmothers made and in the ways of dress on our streets. We should learn to see aesthetic worth in the photographs that we all take and hang up on our walls (to cite just a few examples). The most interesting art is often that which exists outside of the standard venues of high culture and on the periphery of capitalism.

In short, apprenticeship in our age entails the recognition of the limits of our own understandings as well as a recognition of the amount that we have to learn from others. It demands humility with respect to what we know. There is a great deal to learn; in fact, if we accept Heidegger's notion of the artwork as that which opens up a world, then there is no limit to the amount that we can learn.

There is no easy answer to the question of how to decide whether a critic is merely reading his or her own agenda into a work of art. It is true that hooks is very concerned in all of her writings about the suffering of people of color. She finds that Basquiat's work addresses her own concerns, but she is able to explain, in a manner that seems attentive to the works she interprets, why she finds the pain of African Americans invoked in the work of Basquiat. Heidegger is famous or infamous for interpreting other philosophers in ways that advance his own ideas but are often blatantly at odds with what the author actually wrote. Even if Shapiro is too facile in attributing the shoes to Van Gogh, he does, I find, underline the hijacking involved in Heidegger's attribution of the shoes to the Black Forest peasant. In the attempt to understand artworks we owe it to ourselves and to the work to leave the comforts of home. Artworks do open up worlds that cannot be circumscribed by neat rational understandings, but at the same time it is possible to misappropriate and misinterpret works of art by connecting them to impoverished clichés or failing to lace them to the worlds out of which they come. Hooks is not the master of Basquiat's works, but she clearly has important insights that can help those of us who are not African American understand the world out of which these paintings come.

NOTES

1. See Jacques Derrida, *The Truth in Painting*, trans. Geoff Bennington and Ian McLeod (Chicago: University of Chicago Press, 1987). "Restitutions" is the last chapter of this work. For the French text see *La Vérité en Peinture* (Paris: Flammarion, 1978). (Hereafter all references to this work are cited parenthetically in the text as *Truth* and followed first by the page numbers from the English translation and then the page numbers from this French edition.)

2. As John Sallis notes, Heidegger wrote in a letter that in "The origin of the art work" beauty is not thought of in terms or in terms of "'enjoyment,' but rather as a way of shinning . . . , i.e., of truth." Art and beauty, Sallis writes, are to be thought of "in relations to shinning and truth." *Stone* (Bloomington: Indiana University Press, 1994), 98.

3. Martin Heidegger, "Origin of the Work of Art," in *Poetry, Language and Thought* (New York: Harper & Row), 27. For the German text see *Holzwege*, 6th ed. (Frankfurt am Main: Klostermann, 1980), 12. (Hereafter references to this work will be cited parenthetically in the text as "Origin," followed first by the page numbers from the English translation and then the page numbers from this German edition.)

4. I find *das Zeug* very difficult to translate. Joan Stambaugh translates it as "useful thing" in her translation of *Being and Time* (Albany: State University of New York Press, 1996). In John Macquarrie and Edward Robinson's translation of *Being and Time* they translate it as "equipment." They note that there is no precise English equivalent and suggest that it could also be translated as "implement," "instrument," "tool," "gear," or "paraphernalia." They also note that the word can also mean "stuff." *Being and Time* (New York: Harper & Row, 1962), 97. Albert Hofstadter renders it "a piece of equipment" in his translation of "The Origin of the Work of Art," *Philosophies of Art and Beauty* (New York: Random House, 1964). Derrida uses the word *"produit."* "Equipment" and *"produit"* suggest that the shoes are a manufactured product. The German *Zeug* has a very wide range of meanings. Although it can mean "equipment" or "tools" and often refers to "cloth," the first translation that comes to my mind is simply "stuff." Moreover, the word can also be translated as rubbish, trash, or junk and is often used this way. Macquarrie and Robinson argue that "stuff" and the other pejorative connotations are not, for the most part, what Heidegger has in mind in *Being and Time*.

5. Martin Heidegger, *Sein und Zeit* (Tübingen: Max Niemeyer Verlag, 1986), §15.

6. Luc Ferry states, and I think he is correct, that when Heidegger writes that art is the setting-into-work of truth this indicates that, for Heidegger, the work is separated from the artist. The work holds a truth that does not belong to the artist. Ferry writes that for Heidegger the work's essential aspect is to be found in its "preserving of a truth that does not belong to an artist." My question is, does Heidegger's "opening up of the artwork" cause him merely to create a space to read his own agenda onto the work? Luc Ferry, *Homo Aestheticus* (Chicago: University of Chicago Press, 1993), 190.

7. Sallis, *Stone*, 114.

8. Ibid., 115.

9. *Christopher Fynsk, Heidegger: Thought and Historicity* (Ithaca, N.Y.: Cornell University Press, 1968), 132.

10. Ibid., 156.

11. Fynsk also writes that given the work's necessary relation to something outside itself, "it must bear a trace of *Dasein*'s self-reserving finitude." Ibid., 155.

12. Ibid., 169.

13. Heidegger asserts that there is no essential difference between the happening of truth in the artwork and the happening of truth in the act that grounds a state. He writes that truth establishes itself in the act that founds a political state. As the world opens itself it "submits to an historical humanity the question of victory and defeat, blessing and curse, mastery and slavery" (Origin, 63, 49). In bringing out that which is as yet undecided and without measure it discloses the necessity of measure and decisiveness. I find it very strange to tie the artwork and the founding of a political state together as Heidegger does. Political states govern the lives of their citizens, sending soldiers into war, imprisoning people, setting economic policies, educating children, providing health care. Political states need to provide us with stability and a just allocation of resources. Political instability is often deadly in a way that the disruption caused by art rarely is. Artworks shake up our normal way of thinking and lead to new insights, but when the political state changes drastically people are often left unable to provide for their most basic needs. In the 1930s Heidegger, at least for a time, looked to Nazism to rejuvenate the German state to provide for an opening up of the political world akin to the opening up that art provides for the spiritual world. It is, at the very least, a testament to Heidegger's political naivete to equate works of art and politics in this way.

14. This does not mean that a work will find its preservers at once or perish. A work of art cannot exist without preservers, but at times a work may be "only waiting for its preservers *(Bewahrenden)* . . . [it] only pleads and waits for them to enter into its truth" (Origin, 67, 54). Heidegger writes that Hölderlin is still waiting for the Germans to be the preservers of his poetry.

15. Robert Bernasconi's very rich article, "The Greatness of the Work of Art," is to a large extent what prompted me to pay attention to the role that Heidegger's politics plays in this article. In particular, it was Bernasconi's article that led me to think about political implications of Heidegger's comments on the role of preservers of works of art. He handles

this issue over the development of the three versions of the essay in much greater detail than I do here. See *Heidegger in Question: The Art of Existing* (Atlantic Highlands, N.J.: Humanities Press, 1993).

16. Derrida does not go into how Heidegger's changes in this essay correspond with the changing political situation. For an analysis of how "The Origin of the Work of Art" changes, see Robert Bernasconi, "The Greatness of the Work of Art," in *Heidegger in Question*.

17. bell hooks, *Art on My Mind* (New York: The New Press, 1995), 36. (Hereafter references to this work will be cited parenthetically in the text as "hooks.")

18. According to Heidegger, one place that truth does not happen is in science. Science merely cultivates a previously opened domain of truth (Origin, 62, 50).

19. This notion of apprenticeship is borrowed from Elizabeth Spelman, *Inessential Woman* (Boston: Beacon Press, 1988). In particular, see pages 180–82. She has in turn taken it from Jean-Paul Sartre's early work, *Psychology of Imagination* (Secaucus, N.J.: Citadel Press, n.d.). For the original French text, see *L'Imaginaire: Psychologie Phénoménologique de L'Imagination* (Paris: Gallimard, 1940). (Hereafter references to Sartre's text give the English title and then the page number of first this English translation and then this French edition.)

20. Spelman, *Inessential Woman*, 181.

21. *Psychology of the Imagination*, 10, 19.

22. Cornel West, *Race Matters* (New York: Vintage, 1994), 119.

4

ADORNO, JAZZ, AND THE LIMITS OF APPRENTICESHIP

That which we do not know well, we often judge by that which we do know. Adorno knew a great deal about art in general and music in particular, and he was not entirely ignorant of jazz. He certainly knew a great deal about what Germans in the twenties and thirties most commonly associated with jazz, and he even had some sense that there were other kinds of jazz in the United States. One might excuse his first writings on jazz—from 1934 and 1936—given Germany's cultural isolation, but what of the writings from the 1950s, essays written after his sojourn in the United States and after several pointed challenges to his earlier writings? *Aesthetic Theory*, one of the masterpieces of art theory, written in the 1960s, continues to disparage jazz even as it makes wonderful reading about the irreducible enigmas of art. Perhaps this is what "masterpieces" are often destined to do.

Adorno studied jazz, but he never approached it with the humility of an apprentice. Even if one does, there is no guarantee that one will come to love that which one studies. In questions of food we seem to understand that all things will not taste good to all people, but in art we often dismiss the art of others if it rubs against our taste. For my purposes art encompasses many things, from the blues to academically trained painters. Not all art forms appeal to all people. Art is deeply imbedded in our social worlds, and therefore the more we learn about the social worlds out of which artworks come, the better our chance of understanding someone else's art. Derrida, following on Heidegger, has provided us with a model of apprenticeship. Derrida is very clear that artworks can never be interpreted completely. There will always be some remainder; artworks will always exceed our attempts to frame them. Artworks, as Heidegger suggests, do open up worlds, and that makes it impossible for anyone to have complete mastery of them. But Derrida clearly studied the paintings of Van Gogh more intensely than Heidegger did, and he studied Heidegger's thought more than Shapiro did. Some know more than others, and some have worked harder at trying to understand, but no one knows it all.

For Adorno, great art is disruptive and unsettling and therefore always challenges our ability to understand it. Art that is easily understood ceases to be interesting, not only for Adorno, but for myself as well. Like Adorno, I am not arguing that understanding art is easy or that complete understanding is possible. Adorno emphasizes that art is an enigma but not an unapproachable enigma, nor an esoteric realm reserved for the initiated. Even more, art demands explanation, and it is this putting of art into thought (Adorno refers to this as the spiritualization of art) that makes possible, in my estimation, the understanding of art across cultural divides. Adorno has analyzed the relationship between thought and art perhaps more deeply than any other philosopher in the West. And he knew more about "high" art than almost all other Western philosophers. Analyzing some of his earlier essays as well as his final uncompleted *Aesthetic Theory* will help us to explore further the relationship between art and understanding.

I will examine not only the thought of Adorno, but the "case" of Adorno as well. In now famous—or infamous—essays, as well as in fleeting references in *Aesthetic Theory*, Adorno dismisses jazz. When is the failure of a work of art or a genre of art to move us a sign of our failing or our inability to appreciate otherness? Adorno certainly understood something of American culture. His critiques of the culture industry remain remarkably relevant. But Adorno's writings on jazz demonstrate how far he was from apprenticeship in his writing on this subject. His remarks on jazz are broad and uninformed. They are not at all worthy of a thinker who is devoted to seeing the truth of the particular. In his attempt to expose what he saw as jazz's conformity to established norms, he falls short of his own best insights and yields to a positivism that so much of his philosophical energy is devoted to combating.

I will not refute his critique of jazz in any great detail, in part because others have already done this and also because I do not have the musical expertise.[1] I am assuming that others are right about Adorno's failure to give jazz its due. Precisely because art is so difficult to understand, we must be particularly careful when trying to understand the art that comes out of cultures that we do not know. Adorno was not ignorant of the United States; he was familiar with racism in America. As James Harding notes, when Joachim-Ernst Berendt, writing on Adorno's criticisms of jazz, accused Adorno of implicit racism, Adorno replied that he had written the most important study of racism in the United States in recent times, *The Authoritarian Personality*.[2] Inasmuch as Adorno is a brilliant theoretician of art who genuinely advances our understanding of art theory, he is also an excellent example of someone who knew something about the art form that he was criticizing, but he did not know as much as he thought he did. Most troubling, Adorno did not use his sojourn in the United States to research jazz in greater detail before writing his later works on jazz. His early writings were heavily influenced by his experience of German "jazz." Even if one avoids a technical debate about the merits of Adorno's critique of jazz one can show that once formed, his critical appraisal remained unchanged. Adorno never took advantage of the opportunity to study and experience the new emerging jazz of the 1940s and 1950s. As Harry Cooper writes, "his own crystallized categories determine his experience of music in advance."[3] Adorno clearly lacked the humility of an apprentice. This is perhaps understandable when he was analyzing that which he knew well, but it is obvious that he never studied jazz seriously. To be arrogant and uninformed is a particularly bad combination. I begin by describing Adorno's contributions to the understanding of the enigma of art and then proceed to examine, in more detail, the ways in which Adorno's critique of jazz fell short of apprenticeship.

ART, INTUITION, AND THOUGHT

For Adorno, art always implies a difference between artwork and reality. Quoting Schoenberg, Adorno notes that "one paints a painting, not what it represents" (AT, 4, 14).[4] This is a point that Derrida makes, as we noted in the last chapter, and that both Shapiro and Heidegger at times forget. In the heat of their debate both Shapiro and Heidegger forget one of the most basic "truths" of aesthetics, namely that they are writing about a painting of shoes and that the work of art is never equal to any real pair of shoes. This difference between artwork and empirical reality that is automatically clear in the artwork represents for Adorno the positive moment in art. On the other hand, art is subject to the same kinds of manipulations or, to put it more strongly, perversions that affect everything else in society. Adorno writes that art has a double character: It is both autonomous and a *"fait social"* (social fact) (AT, 5,16). He calls artworks "windowless monads" that represent what they are not. They are separate from the empirical world and yet they are subject to the same dialectical processes that govern the outside world. They both recuperate and neutralize what was once directly and literally experienced.[5] In *Prisms*, Adorno writes that an artwork is neither a "reflection of the soul nor the embodiment of a Platonic Idea. It is . . . a force field between subject and object."[6] Artworks for Adorno must be understood within their social context, but, of course, this is only one element of the work of art (AT, 180, 269). Artworks participate in enlightenment because they do not lie; they present themselves as artworks. The objective world motivates art, but the world will always be separate from the art it motivates. In short, for Adorno art has the great advantage that it does not pretend to be an objective accounting of the world. At the same time, art is never completely divorced from the world. The unsolved antagonisms of reality return in the artwork as the immanent problem of their form (AT, 6, 16). The problem with the claim "art for art's sake" is that it fails to see that art is always in relationship with empirical reality.

Art inherits the notion of revelation from theology. Artworks are in some sense a revelation, and yet if the revelatory element is overemphasized then art is contaminated with the "unreflective repetition of its fetish character at the level of history" (AT, 106, 162). If all traces of revelation are banished from artworks then they become simply the repetition of what is. In other words, we must be careful about assuming that art offers us a clear insight into a better world. Art, like everything else, is a product of the time out of which it comes. The utopian moment in art is not the vision it offers for the future but the disruption that it offers in the present.

Adorno claims that rational and irrational theories of art are equally misguided. Art is rationality that criticizes rationality without abandoning it. His reasons for claiming that art is rational are not as developed as his reasons for claiming that art is not rational. Adorno argues that art, like all human activity, is entangled in the social totality and therefore it cannot be irrational. He is deeply committed to the understanding of the social worlds out of which humans come and cannot entertain the notion that art, or any other social activity, cannot be explained. But neither is art merely reducible to rational principles. Rationality is the organizing element of the work of art (AT, 55, 87), but unlike the organizing principle of the administered world, the organization of the artwork allows for the expression of that which the administrated world represses. Typically rationality is used in an effort to dominate. It is used as a means to control. Adorno envisions a rationality that would be an end rather than a means. This is why he claims that the rational element in the artwork is an end.

Artworks offer a corrective to scientific understandings of the world.[7] The measure of the truth of artworks is the extent to which they absorb "into their immediate necessity what is not identical with the concept" (AT, 101, 155). Concepts package our world too neatly. They force the particular to come under the umbrella of the general and thereby do not do justice to the particular. As we will see, Adorno's writings on jazz dramatically show that it is much easier to identify this problem in the abstract than to avoid it. It is precisely this problem of false subsumption that happens in Adorno's critique of jazz.

Adorno writes that the purposiveness of artworks requires the unpurposive. Although the talk of purposiveness reminds us of Kant, this is only partly Kantian. Adorno and Kant agree that the artwork's lack of purposiveness takes it out of the normal economy of everyday objects. For Kant "purposiveness without a purpose" means that aesthetic pleasure is not tied to the object's utility. For Adorno, the artwork's lack of purposiveness refers to its refusal to function in a scientific way. Indeed, the work of art points to that which conceptual understanding cannot grasp. Artworks puncture reason's claims to totality. Adorno does not argue that art is purely illusory. He criticizes some artworks for becoming "canvas and mere tones" or declining into "happenings" (AT, 103, 158). This art has lost touch with reality. Adorno privileges innovation in his aesthetics, but this is not the *sum bonum* for the determination of aesthetic worth. He believes that Dada became nothing more than radicalized subjectivity. It became detached from society and lost all social resonance. At the point when art loses all contact with social reality it becomes "completely impoverished" (AT, 29–30, 51–52).

Every artwork, according to Adorno, is *Schein*, a word that can be translated as appearance, semblance, or shine. In the first place it is semblance with respect to the real. Adorno refers to reality as antagonistic, and when compared to reality it is immediately apparent that the unified artwork is merely a semblance. Artworks are also semblance with respect to themselves, for there is always and inevitably something false about the unity of art. Every good analysis of an artwork shows this. There is, Adorno writes, a sadness or melancholy associated with art (AT, 105, 161). This sadness arises because the meaning of the work of art is always bound up in semblance. The work of art sighs and says "oh if only it were so." Art must be responsive to the empirical world, according to Adorno, and yet it must also never forget it is separate from the empirical, that it is semblance. The redemption of semblance is central to aesthetics. If it seems a stretch to say that Nietzsche sometimes could sing the blues, how much more contrived would it be to claim that Adorno sometimes sings them as well? The blues is replete with social analyses and with sighs that say "if only it were so." As Angela Davis has shown, the blues offers commentary, analyses, and a hope that the world might change, and this is at the heart of what Adorno hoped that art would provide.

SPIRIT (*GEIST*) AND MIMESIS

The spiritualization of art gives the lie to the notion that aesthetics, in the words of Kant, can be reduced to our feelings as opposed to our intellect. This is not, however, to say that for Adorno art is devoid of intuition. Art without intuition turns into theory pure and simple. Overemphasis on intuition leads one into the bourgeois posture of affirming the status quo. In other words, devoid of spirit the supposedly "purely intuited" often is nothing more than a way to affirm the prevailing aesthetic wisdom. An overemphasis on spirit leads aesthetics to think of itself as science. The doctrine of intuition, according to Adorno, underlines that art cannot be reduced to the concept. But precisely because art struggles against conceptualization it requires concepts (AT, 96, 148). Adorno writes that, "The untruth against which art goes is not rationality, but rationality's stubborn opposition to the particular" (AT, 98, 151). He even goes so far as to say that the profundity of artworks is measured by their ability to carry out tensions that are inherent in their intellectual elements. Artworks can heal the wounds that abstractions have wrought only by increasing abstractions. Art, for Adorno, is essentially spiritual.

Adorno enunciates what he refers to as the "criterion of success" for the spiritualization of art. This process is successful when art is capable of appropriating into its language of form that which bourgeois society has ostracized. In so doing art reveals that nature that has been stigmatized. Spiritualization does not take place through art articulating any particular ideas. Rather spiritualization occurs through the power with which art burst through the intentionless and idea-hostile layers (AT, 93, 144). This is one of the reasons that art is attracted, according to Adorno, to the forbidden. It is also why Adorno endorses Karl Kraus's claim that art introduces chaos into society rather than bringing order. In art, chaos and spirit converge to reject the slickly polished representation of existence. But after having emphasized the disruptive nature of art, Adorno cannot leave it there. However far Adorno sees spiritualization as removing art from the show that entertains, art is not only disruption. If art divests itself of every trace of showiness it is no longer art and it will soon die. That is to say, art that loses all sense of show risks ending up as the reaffirmation and reflection of what is.

Contrary to Plato's claim that the semblance of art comes from art's tie to the sensory world, in fact art's semblance originates in its spiritual essence (*Geist*). But according to Adorno, artworks also contain a mimetic element, and this helps to explain why they cannot be reduced to the rational or the spiritual. As Miriam Hansen writes, for Adorno, mimesis differs from the traditional Platonic notion. It involves a "nonobjectifying interchange with the other . . . it assumes a critical and corrective function vis-à-vis instrumental rationality."[8] Adorno defines mimesis as "the nonconceptional affinity of the subjectively produced with its unposited (*nicht Gesetzten*) other" (AT, 54, 86–87).[9] In other words, art is produced subjectively as opposed to objectively. It does not pretend to be an objective portrayal of the world. Yet this subjectively produced art has an affinity—a nonconceptional affinity—with that which goes beyond the artist. The unposited is that which the artist has not created. In another place, Adorno writes that mimetic comportment does not seek to imitate but rather "makes itself the same" (*macht sich selbst gleich*) (AT, 110, 169). Art is the refuge of mimesis. Art uses mimesis as a response to rationality's failure in the administered world. Art that is no longer being for another but rather speaks itself (*spricht an sich*)—this is art's mimetic consummation (AT, 112, 171). The Western world has placed rationality in the service of its attempts at domination. It has reduced rationality to a means. Through mimesis art tries to get at that which the use of rationality as a means has obscured.

Mimesis is an extremely important notion for Adorno's aesthetic theory. Without it, his theory would risk collapsing into Hegelianism. Hegel haunts *Aesthetic Theory*. There are almost twice as many references to him as there are to Kant, the second most often cited thinker in this work. Adorno's notion of mimesis is a very strange one. I do not understand how affinity can be established outside of concepts. I also do not understand how art can make itself the same nor how it can speak itself. Indeed, the fact that art cannot make itself the same—that there is always something artificial about art—is what led Adorno to claim that melancholy is always associated with art. Most compelling in Adorno's aesthetic theory is his insistence that art both needs explanation and yet can never be fully explained. He does not need to introduce mimesis to escape Hegel. He can do it simply by refusing to allow reason its claim to the absolute truth of art. Adorno would have us believe that the mimetic is that which goes beyond the illusoriness of spirit's semblance and connects art to that which is beyond spirit.

Adorno gives three reasons for spirit's illusoriness: It is separated from its other, it makes itself independent in relationship to its other, and it is intangible in its being for itself and therefore illusory (*ein Scheinhaftes*) (AT, 108, 165). In other words, spirit is separated from that which it tries to categorize. In its attempts to categorize that which is not spirit, it inevitably falls short of its object. Second, spirit is illusory because it takes on a life of its own; our descriptions disguise themselves as reality, replacing that which they purport to describe. Finally, spirit is in and of itself intangible. Yet reality, for Adorno, is always mediated through spirit, and this holds true for artworks as well. He labels as nothing less than superstition the idea that art can speak directly without the mediation of spirit (AT, 90, 140). According to Adorno, it was believed by some that elementary colors or sounds said something directly, without the mediation of spirit, but this is patently false.

Adorno goes to great lengths to separate his notion of spirit from Hegel. He writes that the idealist's notions of spirit are wrong. The spiritual element of art is "the mimetic impulse fixated as totality" (*der festgebannte mimetische Impuls als Totalität*) (AT, 90, 139). I do not know what this means. If, for Adorno, the mimetic is, as I have already said, the "nonconceptional affinity of the subjectively produced with its unposited (*nicht Gesetzten*) other" (AT, 54, 86–87), then how are we to envision this nonconceptual affinity as a totality? How can a totality be nonconceptual? And Adorno does not do much to help us understand how his notion of mimesis could be understood as a totality. Instead he continues his argument by asserting that art always exists within a context and can never be understood outside that context. In modern art colors, sounds, and words have been set free. In other words, paintings may now be abstract, music may be atonal. It may seem as if these colors and tones express something in themselves, but this is not the case. These things mean something because of their context. It is superstition to believe that the color red means something in and of itself. Adorno is trying to walk a line between idealism and realism. Hegel is wrong to reduce art entirely to spirit. Art is spirit and mimesis, but Adorno does believe that all art is mediated through the realm of spirit. Spiritualization works both against and with art. By virtue of its alliance with the "mimetic taboo" spirit works against art; that is to say, spirit seeks to banish the notion that mimesis is possible and thereby, according to Adorno, works against art. At the same time, spirit works toward the identification of the artwork with itself. It therefore excludes that which is heterogenous and strengthens art's mimetic moment. "Only radically spiritualized art is still possible, all other is childish." Rarely content to leave a statement unmodified, Adorno then adds "the aspect of the childish, however, appears to stick to the mere existence of art" (AT, 92, 142). Spirit is both essential to art and not sufficient.

If Adorno is right that spirit is essential to art, then there is hope, I believe, that art can be understood across cultural divides. Understanding each other across cultural divides is rarely easy, but to the extent that we can conceptualize it is possible to share our ideas with others, even those whose experiences are very different from our own. Art is harder to understand than other types of spirit—for example, art is harder to understand than scientific knowing—because it often disrupts our traditional ways of understanding. But even this disruption, Adorno suggests and I would agree, is a spiritual process. Even while undermining abstraction and pointing out the inevitable failings of rationality, art relies on abstraction as well. We can only understand art to the extent that we conceptualize, but this is not to say that we will ever completely understand it. Derrida, Adorno, and for that matter Heidegger, all agree that our understanding of art is never without remainder. We understand art, but we never understand it completely.

ART: THE UNENDING ENIGMA THAT REQUIRES UNENDING INTERPRETATION

For Adorno the claim that consciousness kills art is "a foolish cliché" (AT, 174, 260). Even the power of reflection to dismantle is, Adorno believes, very helpful. In the act of dismantling, consciousness has the ability to exclude or modify that which is inadequate or incoherent in the work of art. What is to be avoided is consciousness directing art from outside of the work and thereby violating the work. Artworks, Adorno writes, must go where they want to go, and reflection can follow them. It is this aspect of art that makes it particularly susceptible to misunderstanding across cultural borders. It is much easier to fit the artwork into our world than to do the work of understanding its place in worlds that are unfamiliar to us.

For Adorno, interpretation, commentary, and critique are not only the ways that we interpret works of art; these three are essential for the very construction of the work of art. He writes that artworks are constantly becoming, and interpretation, commentary, and critique are the forms in which this process of becoming crystallizes. It is through these forms that the truth of the work of art must be understood, and therefore they are also useful to pare away from the artwork that which is false. For Adorno it is through these three forms that the truth of the work of art unfolds; therefore these forms must be refined—actually, he writes that they must "sharpen" themselves until they become philosophical (AT, 194, 288).

There are times when Adorno seems to be arguing that works of art are always inevitably enigmas that cannot be deciphered. Or if they are to be deciphered, then it is only their formal aspects that can be delineated. Adorno writes that any artwork that believes it is in possession of its content is naive. The more one reflects on a work of art the more opaque the artwork becomes. "With the increase in reflection and through its increased power the content obscures itself" (AT, 27, 47). We cannot "squeeze the message" out of great works of art, be they Shakespeare or Beckett. Beckett both refuses to interpret his art and at the same time is highly conscious of his work's technical aspects and the implications of his theatrical and linguistic innovations. This does not mean that Adorno advocates doing away with reflection or the analysis of art. Adorno writes that the darkness associated with artworks is the darkness of the new. It must be interpreted, rather than assuming that this darkness can be replaced with "the clarity of meaning." Instead of naively assuming that thought can illuminate art, Adorno calls upon aesthetic thought to exercise "second reflection" (*Zweite Reflexion*). Second reflection counteracts the tendency that places too much emphasis on the intentions of the artists when interpreting works of art. Second reflection investigates the artwork in considerable detail, but it focuses on the modes of operation (*Verfahrungsweise*) of the artwork, which are the language of art in its widest sense. At the same time, second reflection aims at "blindness" (AT, 27, 47). Beckett's refusal to interpret his work should not be understood as a subjective quirk of a particular artist. Adorno claims that we must give up the notion that the content of artworks can be equated with reason. We must interpret the darkness that inevitably surrounds great works of art, but this darkness can never be eliminated. Indeed, according to Adorno, the enigma of artworks points toward a solution, but the solution can only be found by philosophical reflection (AT, 128, 192). Great artists, according to Adorno, never desire to interpret their works (AT, 55, 87).

Art in itself is enigmatic for Adorno, but there is a difference between understanding the enigmatic character of art in general and the enigma of individual works of art. The process of understanding the enigma of a particular work of art never ends. Adorno writes that "Artworks that are understood and explained completely are not artworks at all" (AT, 121, 185). He compares art to a rainbow: When one gets too close, it disappears. He claims that music is prototypical of all art in that it is at the same time both completely puzzling and completely evident. Even successfully interpreted works of art want to be understood further. Imagination and spiritualization provide the keys to the understanding of artworks, according to Adorno. He writes that imagination provides both the most complete and the most deceptive surrogate for understanding works of art. As an example of how the imagination helps us to understand art, Adorno cites the case where one is capable of imagining music without having heard it. But in calling imagination a surrogate, I take Adorno to be saying that the real business of understanding art falls to spiritualization. The goal is not to do away with the enigma of art nor to come closer to a conceptual understanding of the enigma of art. It is rather to make the enigma of art concrete (AT, 122, 185). It is spiritualization that can do this.

Trying to sort out what Adorno means by all of this is still another enigma, but he gives us an example to illustrate his notion of how to interpret works of art. He writes that when Brecht and William Carlos Williams sabotage the poetic and approximate an empirical report they are by no means actually giving an empirical report. Judgments are like artworks in that they are syntheses; however, the syntheses of artworks do not result in judgments. Adorno also illustrates his understanding of the enigma of art by interpreting the poem "Mousetrap Rhyme" by Edvard Mörike:

> Little guest, little house.
> Dearest mouseline, or mouse,
> boldly pay us a visit tonight
> as the moon shines bright!
> But close the door behind you,
> you hear?
> Thereby be careful of your little tail!
> After dinner we will sing
> After dinner we will spring
> And we will do a little dance:
> Swish Swish!
> My old cat will probably dance with. (AT, 123–24, 187–88)

Adorno writes that the poem can be interpreted as an expression of the sadism that our culture has inflicted upon mice. The poem, using the language of children, invites a mouse to trap itself. Adorno believes that this last line may be read as a child's taunting of the mouse, or it may be understood as a naive child's vision of a child, mouse, and cat dancing. To say that the last line can only be a taunt is to ignore the poem's social and political content. Adorno claims that the poem is more than a nonjudgmental reflex of language on "an abominable, socially practiced ritual." It is more than simply the glorification of the brutality of this ritual, because the poem subordinates itself to the ritual (*sich einordnet*). By making it seem as though there were no alternative to this mouse-catching ritual, the poem criticizes it. It turns the self-evidence of the ritual into a indictment. The poem judges by "abstaining from judgment" (AT,

124, 188). The poem's form sublates its basic convictions and makes the poem infinite.

I am sympathetic to Adorno's claim that artworks do not admit of easy interpretations, but what is striking about his interpretation of this work is the assertion that the poem uses the sadism involved in the practice of trapping mice to comment on the barbarity of bourgeois culture. He clearly believes the poem judges society. Even on his own reading, it is not the unending enigma that he proclaims all artworks are. For Adorno, artworks are, in theory, question marks, but there seems to be no question that this poem speaks to the brutality of Western society. Adorno might reply that the poem remains enigmatic in terms of its truth content. The poem raises the question of the brutality of humans, but it does not state unequivocally that humans are brutal nor does it explicitly condemn the practice of trapping mice or link this practice to any societal criticism. It implies all of this without stating it directly.

Adorno says something similar about Picasso's *Guernica*. He prefaces his comments on the painting by claiming that it is difficult for works of art to obtain power in the contemporary world. Art is threatened not only by being co-opted by the administrative world; if it holds itself too far outside of the world it risks being totally irrelevant. The central criterion for art is "the power of expression through whose tension the artwork with wordless gestures becomes eloquent" (AT, 237, 353). As an example of this kind of power Adorno cites *Guernica*. It is precisely its lack of realism and its inhuman construction that allows it to achieve a powerful and unmistakable expression of the horror of the bombing. Culture has a powerful role to play in checking barbarism. Furthermore, there is a utopian moment in art. The hope for not only life, but a decent life, is an echo that "rings in every authentic artwork" (AT, 252, 374).

Genuine artworks never have clear messages and therefore cannot be engaged. Adorno's resistance to politically engaged art is well known and well documented. Engaged art or art that protests explicitly assimilates itself to the reality against which it protests. He rejected the notion of committed art in an essay that he wrote against Sartre and Brecht called "Commitment."[10] There he argues that the current state of things is such that all works of literature that are overtly political "merely assimilate themselves to the brute existence against which they protest" (AP, 177). By contrast, when works "no longer speak as though they were reporting facts, hairs begin to bristle" (AP, 180). Truly revolutionary art disrupts our current notions of coherence as well as the commonly accepted "facts." This does not mean that for Adorno all art that is disruptive in this way is valued. He admits that some modernist works that challenge traditional forms of meaning can slide into "an empty juggling with meaning"

(AP, 191). There are no clear criteria to tell us when art has slipped into this empty juggling. All art, even disruptive art, relies on the reality that it disrupts to some extent. It could not exist without its opponent. Beckett is praised in the essay on commitment because he is both avant-garde and at the same time his plays and novels are "about what everyone knows and no one will admit." Beckett offers us a minimal promise of happiness but only at the cost of "total dislocation to the point of wordlessness" (AP, 191). Beckett and Kafka explode from the inside what committed art attacks externally and therefore only appears to attack. Once Kafka has rolled over you, any chance for peace with the world is gone. In other words, the experience of really reading Kafka is so unsettling that it is akin to being rolled over by a bulldozer. If Kafka is truly appreciated, then he will unsettle us to the extent that we will never really be at peace with the world again.

Adorno employs the word *autonomous* to describe the art that he champions.[11] He claims that the aesthetic object seen as "pure refiguration" guards against the introduction of consumption and false harmony into the artwork. Autonomous works are governed by their own inherent structures as opposed to the totality of effects that govern committed art. This leads Adorno to label autonomous works "knowledge as non-conceptual objects." This ability to disrupt is the source of autonomous art's nobility (AP, 193). In this earlier essay Adorno is not even ready to admit that a mixture of disruptive form and progressive content is desirable. It is form alone that counts for him. It is precisely because works of art are "eminently constructed and produced objects" that they point the way to the construction of the just life (AP, 194). Autonomous artworks, however, are not independent of the time and place where they arose. Art should be autonomous in the sense that it is not the purveyor of a predetermined political message.

APPRENTICESHIP AND CROSS-CULTURAL UNDERSTANDING

Following Adorno, I believe that art can and should be disruptive. Art is not fully accessible to the rational but not entirely divorced from it either. We can understand art, even art that seems very foreign to us, even if we do not understand it completely. Art is embedded in its social reality. Art cries out for interpretation. But what do we say when a perceptive critic like Adorno turns toward an art that is deeply appreciated not only within the African-American community, but by many others as well—namely jazz—and derides it as "perennial fashion"? I am not saying that the understanding of one another's art will lead us all to feel the same way about art. Nor will the understanding of one another's art lead us all to a similar evaluation of the work of art, and understanding does not mean that we will like or even respect a work or genre of art. Adorno is right, in my opinion, that our understanding of art is never final. We have already seen that even within what may appear to some outside observers as heterogenous communities, people feel about and evaluate artworks very differently. As we saw in chapter 1, there is no unitary African-American perspective on the work of Horace Pippen, nor a unitary white perspective on the work of Jackson Pollock. But Adorno's comments on jazz do not, in my opinion, evidence an understanding of jazz. He dismisses jazz—or more precisely, he appropriates jazz to serve as an example of corrupt bourgeois culture.[12]

Adorno's writings on jazz span several decades.[13] He occasionally suggests that jazz might be in some small way subversive, but for the most part Adorno characterizes it in overwhelmingly negative terms.[14] Leaving aside the question of whether we agree with his criteria for judging art, the ease with which jazz conforms to his definition of perennial fashion also suggests that his understanding is a caricature. In his rush to make jazz into an example of what he detests about popular culture, he misses the chance to understand much about the art he denigrates. Jazz became merely a cog in his system to explain the decadence of twentieth-century capitalism. Adorno's writing on jazz and Heidegger's comments on Van Gogh's shoes express a similar failure. Both use art—appropriate it to their philosophical ends—and thereby fail to give it its due.

In fact, the situation is more complicated than it at first seems. J. Bradford Robinson argues persuasively that Adorno, in the 1930s, knew more about jazz than almost anyone else in Germany.[15] Robinson does a remarkable job of outlining the reception of jazz in Germany, arguing that of German critics, only Adorno was able to distinguish between jazz that originated in the United States and the various musical forms that were often associated with jazz in Germany. Nonetheless, for Adorno, at least until the 1960s, even the word jazz did not mean what it does for us today. The word meant for him "popular music—the syncopated dance music of the 1920s and the big band music of the 1930s and 1940s."[16] Robinson reminds us that for most of the 1920s it was difficult for Germans to have any contact with jazz from the United States. At first Germany was isolated because of the Allied blockade, then hyperinflation discouraged artists from going to Germany and record companies from selling there. German "jazz" was created by German musicians who had only vague notions of jazz and therefore it was based primarily on German commercial music.[17] Adorno himself admits, in the preface he wrote to volume 17 of his collected works, that his early essay "On Jazz" demonstrates a lack of understanding of the "specifically American aspects of jazz."[18] He seems unaware of the extent to which all of his later writings demonstrate this same failure.

As is the case with all of his writings on jazz, in his first major essay, "On Jazz," Adorno mentions very few names, Duke Ellington being an exception, but even he is not discussed in any detail. The essay is extremely interesting as a precursor to *Dialectic of the Enlightenment* because it is primarily about the ways in which the culture industry promotes conformity. For example, Adorno argues that the capital behind publishing houses, radio, and film contributes to a limiting of the choices.[19] The suggestion here is that capital is only interested in the success of the product and therefore is adverse to anything out of the ordinary. Adorno then states that the jazz pieces that have had the greatest societal influence have not been those "which show themselves most purely as interference (*Interferenz*)"[20]—that is to say those which interfere in the working of capitalist society. It is rather the "technically arrested simplistic dances" that have been most influential. This passage is important for several reasons. It shows that Adorno realized that not all jazz is purely commercial, but it also shows that Adorno assumed that most commercially successful jazz was dance music, something that even in the thirties was not the case.

As Robinson points out, once Adorno did encounter American jazz firsthand, or at least had the opportunity to encounter it, he did not change his views that jazz was a derivative art form. In particular, Robinson notes that Adorno refused to recognize the innovations that jazz from the United States spawned in timbre and rhythm. With regard to the rhythmic construction of jazz, Robinson argues that Adorno constantly overlooked and misjudged the rhythmic possibilities in jazz, even in his later essays.[21] He argues that Adorno did a brilliant job of analyzing Weimar popular music in his essays on jazz but misunderstood the jazz of the United States in several important ways. In other words, Adorno dramatically highlights the danger of having *some* knowledge. Adorno did in fact investigate and study jazz, or at least he studied the jazz that was available to him in Germany in the 1920s and 1930s. The case of Adorno shows that once our opinions are formed they risk becoming recalcitrant. Adorno did have the opportunity to put his earlier judgments to the test, but he continued to insist upon the prejudgments of his earlier essays.

As almost all critics have mentioned, Adorno's critiques are very broad. Even in the later works, names are rarely mentioned.[22] This is perhaps justified given the fleeting references to the subject in *Aesthetic Theory*, but even in "Perennial Fashion—Jazz" this trend at generalization is evident. It is particularly interesting to read "Perennial Fashion—Jazz" in conjunction with "Über Jazz" to see how the later essay is largely derivative of the earlier one. For example, in both essays he compares the follower of jazz to the sadomasochist. In "On Jazz" Adorno writes that the contemporary bourgeoisie (*Bügertum*) knows how to enjoy their alienation. They do not take pleasure in the pathos of distance about which Nietzsche wrote. In other words, for Nietzsche a few select individuals take great joy in separating themselves from the herd, but this is a pleasure that Adorno believes the bourgeoisie no longer understand. Now jazz permeates almost all parts of society. Followers of jazz are damaged victims. They are accorded only damaged goods—goods that are the product of sadomasochism. In the late essay he makes much the same point. In "Perennial Fashion—Jazz" he writes that the supposed vitality of jazz is merely a cover meant to disguise alienation. The jazz fan is like the sadomasochist who secretly admires the oppressor and even secretly derives pleasure from his or her subordination.

Adorno argues that jazz is not at all as unruly as it appears. It rigorously excludes "every unregulated impulse" ("Über Jazz," 79; *Prisms*, 122). "So called improvisations are actually reduced to the more or less feeble rehashing of basic formulas in which the schema shines through at every moment" (*Prisms*, 123).[23] For Adorno there is a positive moment in fashion, namely the extreme transience of whims of fashion. Jazz, however, is perennial fashion—it uses only well-defined tricks, formulas, and clichés. Instead of embracing change, jazz covertly embraces bourgeois stability: "It is though one were to cling convulsively to the 'latest thing' and deny the image of a particular year by refusing to tear off the page of the calendar. Fashion enthrones itself as something lasting and thus sacrifices the dignity of fashion, its transience" (*Prisms*, 123). In other words, unlike fashion, jazz clings to the moment.

In *Aesthetic Theory*, written in the 1960s, Adorno contrasts Beethoven with jazz. Beethoven's music offers the "full experience of outer life returned inward" (AT, 116, 177). Popular music, the category into which jazz falls, is merely a "somatic stimulus" and therefore inhibits rather than promoting aesthetic autonomy (Ibid.). At another point in *Aesthetic Theory* he writes that replacing Beethoven with rock and roll and jazz will not expose the barbarity and profit motive of the culture industry. The supposedly vital and uncorrupted qualities of jazz and rock and roll that are allegedly a sign of the rejection of bourgeois culture are in fact "truly corrupt" (AT, 319–20, 473–74). Jazz promises liberation but is nothing more than the affirmation of the status quo. Adorno writes that when listeners of jazz denigrate something as out of date they are merely protesting because of its "incongruity with the disenchanted world" (AT, 59, 93).

It is sadly ironic that the thinker who wrote *Negative Dialectic* could not interrogate and reformulate his position even when he had the chance to experience this genre firsthand. Adorno is much more compelling when he analyzes particular works or artists whom he knows well. For example, Adorno often criticizes Brecht. Whether or not one agrees with his criticisms of Brecht, it is clear that in these criticisms Adorno knows of what he writes. He is very specific about the problems he sees.[24]

There is much that we cannot know, but if we criticize something we should make every effort to understand that which we critique. This is particularly true if we critique something that comes out of another culture. If, as Adorno suggests, art is always part of a social world, then attempts to understand it must explore the world out of which the art comes as well as the art form. There is little evidence that Adorno devoted much time to the study of jazz in the United States even though he continued to write about it. Adorno did study, intensively, the culture of the United States, but this study, coming after his initial encounter with jazz, did not lead him to reevaluate his assessment. Adorno was not nearly as well informed about jazz as he thought he was. The case of Adorno demonstrates that even intensive study does not guarantee understanding.

Adorno's critique of jazz is not true about a great deal of it, but one of his claims may very well be true about some of it. He reminds us of how easily the art that thinks of itself as subversive is co-opted by what he calls the administrative world. The culture industry does co-opt much of contemporary music, and surely some of that which is today called jazz by the culture industry is little more than a commodity, produced to be sold. Some of what today passes for jazz is, as Lorenzo Simpson suggests, merely the product of the culture industry.[25] For Adorno no artistic production is purely subjective. He writes that although an artwork may appear to be merely subjective "that totem of powers that are dragged into the work of art—that appears to be merely subjective is in fact the potential presence of the collective in the work—according to the measure of available productive powers" (AT, 43, 71). Similarly, artistic expression does not equal pure subjectivity for Adorno. The sign of expression, he writes, is not that artworks communicate the subject, but rather where they "reverberate the proto history of subjectivity" (AT, 111, 172). Even though the subject may perceive itself to be unmediated, it is in fact mediated. That which the subject expresses is, according to Adorno, both personal and a product of the subject's social world.

In spite of their monadological essence, artworks are "moments in the movement of spirit" as well as moments of social reality (AT, 194, 288). Works are not merely products of the past, but it will require a liberated and reconciled humanity to have a proper relationship with both past and contemporary works. Adorno insists that artworks do participate in a historical process, but, at the same time, the historical process must be understood from the perspective of the individual works.

Adorno believes that we must look for the relationship of art to society in terms of the production of art rather than the reception of art. He reminds us that even art that starts out looking revolutionary can quickly find itself very acceptable and neutralized by what he calls the "administrative world." He writes that in the administrative world neutralization of art is universal. To illustrate what he means by this he gives the example of surrealism. Surrealism began as a protest movement against the fetishization of art, but then Salvador Dali became society painter of second rank (AT, 229, 340). The reception of works of art tends to neutralize them. A second example that Adorno cites is how once-revolutionary abstract modern paintings have become accepted to the point where they are hanging in modern hotels and on the walls of the homes of the bourgeois.

In the years since the writing of *Aesthetic Theory* there has been little to dissuade me of the truth of Adorno's critique of the culture industry. The culture industry seems to have an insatiable appetite for marginal phenomena. The fashion industry, for example, reaches out for the grunge look and sells it to the upper class the way they once reached out to take blue jeans from the counterculture and market them as "designer jeans." Adorno reminds us that the culture industry has a remarkable ability to appropriate what was once revolutionary. Clearly analogous things are happening in literary culture. When Sapphire, a young and immensely talented but little-known black poet, receives a million-dollar advance from a publisher, that publishing house is betting on its ability to mass market her books. Similarly, Steven Spielberg packaged *The Color Purple* in such a way as to make it acceptable to the masses. Among other things, he downplayed a lesbian relationship.

Adorno reminds us to consider not just what the artwork becomes but the revolutionary nature of its first appearance. It is important to remember that Adorno also wrote about how the culture industry co-opts "classical works."

Lorenzo Simpson has argued that Adorno lacks the vocabulary to understand jazz properly.[26] I am more inclined to believe that Adorno lacked the caring attentiveness of the apprentice. It is not so much that Adorno's critiques of the culture industry are wrong. Today's culture industry seems to confirm many of the claims Adorno made about the commodification of culture in capitalist society. Jazz was and is more than a cultural commodity, but Adorno never studied jazz seriously enough to realize this. Adorno's failure to seriously study jazz during the eleven years that he spent in the United States is all the more striking given that he spent much of that time in New York, where exciting jazz innovations were occurring.

Even as we reject Adorno's wholesale criticism of jazz we must address the question of the politics of art. When we study the world out of which art comes we must not needlessly narrow it. Derrida shows us in *The Truth in Painting* how "peripheral matters" are involved in the debate between Heidegger and Shapiro. And Adorno emphasizes an even wider range of social factors that belong to the creation and reception of art. It is to the range of political factors that affect art that I now turn.

NOTES

1. See, for example, Harry Cooper, "Replaying Adorno with the Grain," *October* 75 (1996): 99–133; Theodore Gracyk, "Adorno, Jazz, and the Aesthetics of Popular Music," *Musical Quarterly* 76 (Winter 1982): 526–42; James M. Harding, "Adorno, Ellison, and the Critique of Jazz," *Cultural Critique* 31 (1955): 129–58; and William P. Nye, "Theodor Adorno on Jazz: A Critique of Critical Theory," *Popular Music and Society* 12, no. 4 (Winter 1988): 69–73. For a critique of Nye's critique, see Carol V. Hamilton, "All That Jazz Again: Adorno's Sociology of Music," *Popular Music and Society* 15, no. 3 (1991): 31–40. See also J. Brandford Robinson, "The Jazz Essays of Theodor Adorno: Some Thoughts on Jazz Reception in Weimar Germany," *Popular Music* 13, no. 1 (January 1994): 1–25; and Peter Townsend, "Adorno on Jazz: Vienna Versus the Vernacular," *Prose Studies* 11 (1988): 69–88. This last article fails to consider the range of Adorno's writings on jazz. It provides some important critiques of "Perennial Fashion—Jazz," even if some of its attacks on Adorno seem less convincing.

2. Harding, "Adorno, Ellison, and the Critique of Jazz," 136.

3. Cooper, "Replaying Adorno with the Grain," 104.

4. I have made extensive use of Robert Hullot-Kentor's fine translation of Adorno's *Aesthetic Theory* (Minneapolis: University of Minnesota Press, 1997), but the translations given in this chapter have often been modified based on my own reading of the original *Ästhetische Theorie*, 4th ed., edited by Gretel Adorno and Rolf Tiedemann (Frankfurt am Main: Suhrkamp Taschenbuch Verlag). When quoting from this work I use a parenthetical citation (AT) including first the pages from Hullot-Kentor's translation and then the pages from this German edition.

5. As Martin Jay states, the entire Frankfurt School rejected the notion that art is the

product of merely individual creativity. See *The Dialectical Imagination: A History of the Frankfurt School and the Institute of Social Research 1923–50* (Berkeley: University of California Press, 1966), 177.

6. *Prisms*, trans. Samuel and Shierry Weber (Cambridge, Mass.: MIT Press,1983), 184.

7. For Adorno, art "recaptures the proper mimetic relationship between man and nature. In art, unlike more theoretical activities, conceptual domination of the natural world was checked by sensuous receptivity," Martin Jay, *Adorno* (Cambridge, Mass.: Harvard University Press, 1984), 76.

8. Miriam Bratu Hansen, "Mass Culture as Hieroglyphic Writing: Adorno, Derrida, Kracauer," in *The Actuality of Adorno: Critical Essay on Adorno and the Postmodern*, ed. Max Pensky (Albany: State University of New York Press, 1977), 90.

9. The notion of *setzten* is taken out of Hegel's *Logic*. It is particularly prominent in the second book of the *Logic*. It is, for both Hegel and Adorno, integral to the process of reflection, in particular to reflection's alienation from itself.

10. This essay is found in English translation in *Aesthetics and Politics*, edited by Ronald Taylor (London: Verso, 1977), 177–95. All future references to this work are cited as AP followed by the page number from this edition.

11. For a discussion of Adorno's notion of autonomy, see Lambert Zuidervaart, *Adorno's Aesthetic Theory: The Redemption of Illusion* (Cambridge, Mass.: MIT Press, 1994), 80ff.

12. For example, Adorno often writes about the relationship between popular songs and jazz. As Theodore Gracyk notes, much of even Louis Armstrong's best work was not based on popular songs or on either the twelve- or thirty-two-measure songs. He writes that later jazz, such as that of Charlie Parker, is "the very antithesis of entertainment." It is disturbing music that one does not want to hear often. "Adorno, Jazz, and the Aesthetics of Popular Music," 532.

13. His first longer essay on jazz, "Über Jazz," was written under the pseudonym Hektor Rottweiler and published in *Zeitschrift für Sozialforschung* 5, no. 2 (1936). Martin Jay reports that the essay was published under the pseudonym because at the time Adorno still made occasional trips back to Germany (*The Dialectical Imagination*, 185). His other major essay on jazz, "Perennial Fashion," appeared in *Prisms*. The essay was written, according to Jay, in 1953, and the book was published in German in 1955. In addition, Adorno comments on jazz in several shorter essays: "Abschied vom Jazz" (1933), in *Gesammelte Schriften*, vol. 18 (Frankfurt am Mein: Suhrkamp, 1984), 795–99. See also his review of Wilder Hobson's *American Jazz Music* and Winthrop Sargent's *Jazz Hot and Hybrid* in *Studies in Philosophy and Social Science* 9, no. 1 (1941): 169. See also Adorno and Joachim-Ernst Berendt, "Für und Wider Jazz" [For and Against Jazz], *Merkur: Deutsche Zeitschrift für Europäisches Denken* 7, no. 9 (1953): 887–93; and "Jazz," in *Encyclopedia of the Arts*, ed. Dagobert D. Runes and Harry G. Schrickel (New York: Philosophical Library, 1946), 511–13. He makes several brief comments on jazz in *Aesthetic Theory* (AT, 93, 59; 177, 116; 322, 217; 473, 319–320). Adorno's evaluation remains overwhelmingly negative.

14. As Sabine Wilke and Heidi Schlipphacke note, Adorno uses the metaphor of sexual impotence to criticize jazz and Hofmannsthal. Jazz and Hofmannsthal are also said to emas-

culate their listeners. Wilke and Schlipphacke argue that unreconstructed stereotypes of masculinity and femininity have influenced Adorno's schema for determining what are successful works of art. The use of these unreconstructed stereotypes acts against the liberation that Adorno seeks. "Construction of a Gendered Subject: A Feminist Reading of Adorno's Aesthetic Theory," in *The Semblance of Subjectivity: Essays in Adorno's Aesthetic Theory* (Cambridge, Mass.: MIT Press, 1997), 306.

15. J. Bradford Robinson, "The Jazz Essays of Theodor Adorno: Some Thoughts on Jazz Reception in Weimar Germany," *Popular Music* 13, no. 1 (January 1994): 7.

16. Ibid., 9.

17. Ibid., 4.

18. Theodor Adorno, *Musikalische Schriften IV: Moments musicaux Impromptus Gesammelte Schriften,* band 17 (Frankfurt am Main: Suhrkamp Taschenbuch Verlag, 1997), 11.

19. "Über Jazz," in ibid., 80.

20. Ibid.

21. Robinson, "Jazz Essays of Theodor Adorno," 12.

22. As James M. Harding notes, Adorno seems particularly uninformed about developments in jazz in the 1940s; in particular, he never critically engages bebop: "With the exception of his categorical rejections in 1953 and 1962, Adorno displays no knowledge of bebop whatsoever." "Adorno, Ellison, and the Critique of Jazz," *Cultural Critique* 31 (1955): 129–58. Harding argues that Adorno's understanding of jazz came from his conversations in Germany with Mátyás Seiber, a jazz critic during the 1930s, and from his reading of Sargent's *Jazz: Hot and Hybrid,* which was published in 1938.

23. Gracyk suggests that in the thirties when Adorno was developing his views most popular jazz groups did rely on stock arrangements and downplayed improvisation, but even at this time he gives examples of Louis Armstrong, Billie Holiday, and Coleman Hawkins as jazz musicians for whom this was not true. "Adorno, Jazz and Popular Music," 533. He also cites a quotation from Sonny Rollins that one must guard against making jazz "too written . . . because that is what can kill it." Gracyk argues that each jazz performance is an "independent musical work." Ibid., 537.

24. Peter Townsend makes a similar observation, noting that Adorno's critiques of jazz in *Prisms* are not nearly as precise or well informed as his articles on Bach. "Adorno on Jazz: Vienna Versus the Vernacular," *Prose Studies* 11 (1988): 70.

25. Lorenzo C. Simpson, *The Unfinished Project of Modernity* (New York: Routledge, 2001), 54.

26. Simpson, *Unfinished Project of Modernity,* 55.

5

ART AND THE POLITICS OF REPRESENTATION IN THE SOUTH BRONX

At times art seems like such a trivial pursuit. Adorno asks how can one write poetry after Auschwitz. How could we visit galleries as the bombs were falling on Sarajevo, or as 7,000 men were being killed in Sbernicia, or as several hundred thousand were being killed in Rwanda? Or how can we write poetry as millions are dying each year in the underdeveloped world from preventable diseases such as food-borne diseases and malaria? Why go to galleries when so many children in the world's richest nation live in poverty?[1] Is art merely a divertissement? Adorno reminds us that the commandant of Auschwitz went home every night and played Bach for his family. As we drift in and out of galleries, go to concerts, and buy African art for our homes, is this merely a way to forget that in many countries in sub-Saharan Africa 20 percent of children die before reaching the age of five of preventable diseases? Art could be and sometimes is used to dramatize human suffering. Art that serves merely to convey a political message—for example communist realism, favored at one time in the Soviet Union—may be useful as propaganda, but is often distinctly uninspiring.

But there are many ways for art to be uninspiring. Movies are often little more than marketing tools, intimately tied to fast-food outlets, clothes, and automobile sales. Adorno reminds us that even the most abstract art fits comfortably in hotels, and I would add corporate headquarters. I am aware of the dangers of "committed art," that is to say, art that merely serves to convey and proselytize a political message. Those who would insist on an absolute separation of art are misguided because art is always involved in politics. Furthermore, the political content of art does not necessarily detract from its artistic content. For example, as the people of Sarajevo were suffering under the bombardment there was a movement to make Sarajevo the "Cultural Capital of Europe." Each year one city in Europe is named the cultural capital of Europe. Cities use this as an occasion to sponsor a series of exhibitions and artistic festivals and to install art in public places. Berlin, Paris, and a host of other European cities have had this designation for a year. Those arguing for naming Sarajevo as the cultural capital of Europe were trying to use art to bring attention to the suffering of the populace. At the same time, Susan Sontag traveled to Sarajevo to put on a production of *Waiting for Godot*.

I believe that art is more than a divertissement. It is one of the most important ways that humans express themselves about that which cannot be expressed scientifically. To speak with Heidegger, it opens up worlds. If art is to be important it must, among other things, speak to and about the social and political realities in which we live. If art opens worlds, then it will speak to us of the political and economic realities that it finds in those worlds. The opening of the world of Sarajevo of the 1990s is surely a very rich field for artistic expression, and part of what makes it a worthwhile subject is the political realities of that time.

Understanding the art of others is one way that we become aware of the social and political realities of each other's lives. Chinua Achebe's *Things Fall Apart*, Morrison's *Paradise*, and Picasso's *Guernica* are all examples of art that is intimately connected with the political and social realities of its day. Each of these works of art has brought us closer to the suffering of others, without being didactic.[2] Other works tell us of people's joys. These works lead us to contemplate the social and political conditions under which people live, but their messages are not reducible to simple formulas. The first section of this chapter explores how Morrison's *Paradise* speaks of social and political realities without oversimplifying them. She writes of the worlds in which black people live without reducing them to oversimplified clichés.

My concern here is to show that art cannot be divorced from politics. The second section of this chapter looks at the question of art and politics from a different perspective. It underlines how much of what we in the United States and Europe commonly think of as art is deeply involved with the capitalist marketplace. In the United States and Europe not only are commercial art spaces, the music industry, and film deeply intertwined with the workings of our capitalistic society, but museums, orchestras, and other "public institutions" also are increasingly, particularly in the United States, relying on private industry's money. In the United States it is difficult, if not impossible, to go to a major exhibition or performance without hearing about the corporate sponsors. At least some of the influences of such arrangements are obvious. To cite the most infamous example, it is remarkably transparent that tobacco companies use their sponsorship of cultural events as a way to enhance their public image. When a tobacco company sponsors a cultural event it is obviously trying to divert attention from the fact that it is peddling products that are highly addictive and deadly.

Some art may seem to escape some of these capitalist influences by being "publicly financed," but not the most controversial art or the quilt making of my grandmother, although, interestingly, some contemporary quilt makers do receive public funding. Not only the marketplace, but also the state uses art to promote itself. It has been suggested that museums, orchestras, and other cultural institutions funded by the state serve to legitimize the state. At a time when states seem unable to assure many of their citizens basic needs such as employment, health care, and housing, these "great" cultural institutions and productions serve to mask the state's inability to care for its citizens. Other less-cynical voices would point out that cultural institutions such as the Pompidou Center in Paris and the Guggenheim Museum in Bilbao have been used to reinvigorate economically sections of cities and even whole cities.

When we ask about cross-cultural understanding of art, we must do so with the knowledge that art is often used to obscure or else unabashedly promote political and economic ends. The study of this appropriated art will tell us much about the culture industry but little about the life worlds of others. It is the fact that these works do not tell of the social and political realities of people's lives that makes them such useful commodities. Works of art that are more than vehicles for commercial interests will be vitally important to our efforts to understand others because they will be works that open up the worlds of others.

Intimately tied to the capitalist exploitation of culture is the notion of the masterpiece, or the politics of "greatness." What makes us think that some artworks are better than others? Clearly the marketplace plays a role in this. Art museums and exhibitions promote themselves with the claim of showing "great" art. A cultural institution is legitimized to the extent that it exhibits great art. Galleries use greatness to justify their prices. There may well be such a thing as a "great" artwork, but I am increasingly skeptical about this term. Surely some art evidences greater technical skill, but when we say of an artwork that it is a masterpiece we mean something more than that it required great technical skill. Some works do connect very powerfully with my feelings and my intellect, but I recognize that the art that speaks so powerfully to me will not necessarily speak so powerfully to others. To the extent that an artwork opens up worlds, then it is, in my estimation, valuable. I recognize that this is a vague criterion on which to decide the worth of art, but perhaps there is some value to being vague. I want to cast a wide net, but not too wide a net. What matters to me here is to discuss why social and political realities are the legitimate stuff of art. To this end it is important to differentiate between complex engagements with life and instrumental acts designed to be merely marketing tools.

In the third section I explore the politics of interpreting art and of working with images from other cultures. Who does control, and who should control, the interpretation of artworks? I have been arguing that cross-cultural understandings of art are possible, but what are the politics that come into play when, for example, white males from the dominant culture seek to interpret the work of African-American women? I have already argued that we should use caution and humility when interpreting art from another culture, but here I emphasize that we should not be so cautious that we never engage the art of others. Caution and humility are virtues, but like most virtues even they can be overused. As I have already stated, I do believe it is possible to understand art across cultural borders if we study the lifeworld out of which this art comes. I also believe that it is possible to work with images from another culture, but we must ask about the politics of working with images of those who are of different races, genders, and classes. African Americans tell us that there is a long history of whites misusing the images of blacks. One need only think, for example, of the portrayal of blacks in D. W. Griffith's *Birth of a Nation* or the Willie Horton advertisements in George Bush's 1998 election campaign. How do we do this without violating, that is, presenting caricatures of, those with whose images we are working?

All attempts to divorce art from the political end up impoverishing our understanding of art. At the same time, we have not yet developed a sophisticated understanding of the interrelationship of art and politics. In what follows I do not attempt to develop a definitive taxonomy of the ways in which art and politics intersect. Instead, I pursue these three related sets of questions in an attempt to flesh out some of the ways in which art and politics intersect, or rather I explore some of the ways in which both the understanding and the making of art is inevitably intertwined with the political and how this influences our attempts to understand art across cultural borders.

MURDER IN *PARADISE*

I argue in chapter 2 that the bluesy Nietzsche recognizes that life is embedded in social realities. Art is not, as Nietzsche sometimes argues, a product of one's biology, but comes out of the social worlds we inhabit. Instead of asking whether art and politics can mix without reducing art to pedantry, we should ask what the cost to art is when it attempts to divorce itself from the political. Is this divorce even possible? If art is to be more than a mere divertissement, if it is to open up the worlds in which we live, then to divorce art from the political is to divorce art from much of what shapes our lives. Part of what makes Morrison's work so powerful is that she writes about the racism and sexism that so deeply permeate the United States. There are few clear political messages from Morrison's work, but her nuanced engagement with racism and sexism and the effect that this has on African Americans is one of the things that makes her work significant and interesting. Morrison's work cannot be reduced to sexual or racial politics, but these politics clearly infuse her writings as they permeate the lives of African Americans and all others who live in the United States.

Morrison's work is striking for its ability to dissect the horrible toll that racism and sexism exact without yielding to simple platitudes. History can recount the story of a black woman who took the life of her child to keep the child from falling into slavery near Cincinnati. Morrison's novel, *Beloved*, speaks to us of the haunting legacy of that act of infanticide and the institution of slavery. It describes, among other things, not only the haunting of the dead child but the haunting specter of slavery even after it was abolished. At the same time it also speaks of the loving relationship between Sethe and Paul D.

In *Paradise*, Morrison portrays the troubled relationships between men and women in the African American community of Ruby, or more exactly, she portrays the troubled relationship among a group of five women, four of whom we assume are African-American, and the black town nearby. The black town is to some extent prosperous. It prides itself on the fact that doors can be left unlocked and that women can walk down the streets at dusk without fear. Yet it is also a town whose "leading" male citizens brutally murder five women (four of whom are black) who live outside of town. Even though it is set in the 1970s, this novel opens up the world of African-American women in the 1990s. It is the world of the confrontation between Clarence Thomas and Anita Hill, the O. J. Simpson trials, and the rape of Desire Washington by Mike Tyson. It is also the world where black women, as Collins writes, are often stereotyped and demonized as "welfare mothers, matriarchs, mammies and

Jezebels" by whites.³ Within the African-American community, black women are often victimized by the stereotype of the "superstrong black woman." hooks, West, and Kimberlé Crenshaw have given us theoretical accounts of the Hill/Thomas confrontation.⁴ Pearl Cleage writes "objectively" and very powerfully about violence against all women.⁵ Morrison examines these things through her fiction.

The power of Morrison's account in *Paradise* lies, for me, in her ability to tell each of her character's stories in a compelling way. *Paradise* describes the toll that racism and sexism exact on each of these women's lives. Morrison does not idealize any of her characters. One woman, Mavis, not only left her family but also was in part responsible for the death of her young twins. She left them in a locked car on a hot day while she was shopping in a supermarket, and they died a horrible death. Morrison shows how Mavis was overwhelmed by an abusive husband and her attempt to care for her children. Her husband rapes her on a regular basis. The reason for her trip to the supermarket that led to the tragedy was to buy meat for her family's dinner. Her husband insisted that Spam was not a proper meat for his dinner and that she should not leave the babies with him while she went shopping for something else. As her children are dying of heat exhaustion in a parked car with the windows rolled up, Mavis is wandering around in a daze trying to decide what might satiate both her husband's hunger and his anger. Mavis is threatened by not only her husband but also her older rebellious children. Morrison describes a dinnertime conversation in which Mavis's twelve-year-old daughter Sal asks her father about the sharpness of his straight razor: "Is it sharp enough to cut . . . ? And Frank (the father) would answer, "Cut anything from chin hair to gristle" or "Cut the eyelashes off a bedbug," "eliciting peals of laughter from Sal."⁶ Mavis is convinced that her children and husband plan to kill her. As Mavis describes her shopping in the supermarket that led to the death of her twins, one understands how oppressive her life had become.

After the death of her twins, she leaves the family. By chance she ends up living outside of Ruby with four other women and is one of those killed by the "leading" men of the town. As I have already said, there exists, principally among European Americans and the media, what Collins has identified as the myth of the welfare mother. African-American women, the myth suggests, are "content to sit around and collect welfare, shunning work and passing on [their] bad values to [their] offspring."⁷ Among African Americans, Collins has identified another controlling image of the superstrong black mother. This myth suggests that black women are capable of doing it all—raising children and earning money—all without the help of a man. Morrison's *Paradise* explores the realities of African-American women's lives without didacticism. It undermines both the myth of the superstrong black woman and the myth of the welfare mother. It portrays lives marked by catastrophes and sorrow. There are ambiguities about each of Morrison's characters that are not finally resolved. Even though the characters seem to be killed in the first chapter of the book, at the end of the book they seem to be alive. In the midst of the ambiguity stories of pain, suffering, friendship, and struggle are told. Morrison deftly plays her characters against each other. I empathized with the female characters, but the male characters who went out to kill the "deviant" women who lived outside of town were also rich and full. To create characters that show the complexity that the stereotypes obscure is part of the beauty of Morrison's work. Like Faulkner's *As I Lay Dying* and Achebe's *Things Fall Apart*, Morrison's work always leaves us with more questions than answers. To quote from Davis, it reveals "that the social circumstances of black peoples lives produce an endless series of calamities."[8] It also reveals that some of these calamities are inflicted by other African Americans. To write, or paint, or sing of these calamities is a political act. It is also a political act to write or sing of loving relationships between black men and women. To do so counteracts the stereotype of blacks as Jezebels and beasts who, ruled by their appetites, are incapable of loving relationships. In short, her ability to convey something of the complexities of African-American lives without reducing her characters to stereotypes is part of what I find so compelling in Morrison's work.

ART AND THE MARKET

Even if artists are earnestly working toward the creation of art that is not aimed primarily at commercial success, once their work is placed in the marketplace it is subject to all of the manipulations that accompany market forces. In some galleries it is quite obvious that making money is the chief concern. Commercial galleries do not survive if they are not astute about the marketplace. Music is also big business, as is cinema: much of what both these industries produce is transparently aimed at making money. Adorno and Horkheimer's critiques of the culture industry seem in some ways even more true today than they were when *Dialectic of the Enlightenment* was written in the 1940s. Commercial television, with few exceptions, is nothing more than a vehicle for advertising. Its vacuity is obvious. It is a sad commentary on cinema in the United States that it is turning back to old television shows to find inspiration for new movies.

One of the places where *Dialectic of the Enlightenment* may be dated is in its assessment of the culture industry's power. Adorno was convinced that it was a weak industry when compared to heavy manufacturing. In this information age, where the demand for entertainment seems relentless, the culture industry may be more powerful today than it once was.

The state's use of culture to legitimate its ends is in some ways more transparent in Europe than it is in the United States. It is sad and ironic that François Mitterand, the former socialist president of France, is remembered not only for the institutions of high culture that he either renovated or built (for example the Louvre, the Bastille Opera, and the new National Library), but also for the historic rates of unemployment that accompanied his "reign." In a few years we will remember, perhaps, only the monuments.[9] The massive outlays for public projects made by the French socialist government in some ways serve to hide its inability to solve France's economic problems.

Public funding for the arts in the United States is a fraction of what it is in Europe. In the United States, there is such a puritanical distrust of the arts by some conservatives that for several years there have been attempts to cut all funding for the arts from the national government. Into the funding void, however, steps the private sector. Performances and exhibitions are advertising vehicles for their corporate sponsors. More than that, however, they are signs of "good corporate citizenship." Even as companies lay off large numbers of employees, they seek to repair their images by handing out a few crumbs to local art institutions. The tobacco companies have been banned from most forms of advertising, but they are omnipresent and welcome in the arts. National Public Radio, which used to advertise itself as "commercial free," now describes itself as "listener supported." One hears commercials on National Public Radio almost as often as one hears them on commercial television. National Public Radio is particularly attractive to advertisers because of the demographics of its listeners.

The problem with public or private funding for art goes beyond the problem of whether such arrangements censor controversial art. It is true that neither the government nor the private sector is particularly happy about supporting controversial art such as Serrano's *Piss Christ* or Robert Mapplethorpe's explicit homoerotic images.[10] Equally important, particularly in the case of private funding, it supports that which is entertaining in the most vacuous ways. There is increasingly little room in the venues of "high culture" for art that probes and art that is about exploring and trying to understand something of the worlds in which we live. Most television does not even make the pretense of being art. It is not even "pure entertainment." Television is entertainment as marketing tool. It presents us with worlds of the rich and famous so that we might imagine, for a few moments, that we are rich and famous. It cuts every seven minutes to sell us a product that will also help to transport us to this mythical world. As Adorno writes, it not only sells us the dream but also pounds home the message of the powerlessness of individuals. Those in control can take people up into their heaven and just as quickly can throw them out again.[11] The culture industry drives home the message that we are mere objects and that resistance is useless. We can be millionaires if we are lucky, but our efforts are useless.

Television is continuous and seamless marketing. And the commercial art world is often not much different. Corporate money in the arts flows toward that which will reliably draw a crowd: the "established favorites." It brings us the *Nutcracker* at Christmas, the Impressionists ad nauseam, and any other well-established "masterpiece" as long as it is not too controversial. For a section of the bourgeoisie it is important "to have culture." They think it is to be bought for the price of a ticket to the latest blockbuster exhibition. The museum catalogues write about the masterpieces contained in their exhibitions, and after enduring a few minutes in the throngs the satisfied consumers can return to discuss their reactions or, more likely, merely mention their visit, to this "art" and prove their social status.[12]

Art that is not created for a market is often much more powerful than art that is made to be sold. Clearly, some art that has achieved market success remains very powerful. Faulkner and Morrison have both achieved critical and commercial success. I can even still see, on occasion, the power in the Impressionists, in Van Gogh, in the cinema and an opera, even though they have served as beasts of burden to our capitalist system. By this I mean that museums large and small have used the Impressionists and Postimpressionists to pack their galleries, and sponsors of these exhibits have used their sponsorship to sell their images. My point is not to dismiss all commercially successful art; I do not even entirely reject the notion of a masterpiece, although it is obvious that today the term "masterpiece" is, more than anything, a tool used to draw in the crowds. I want to downplay the notion of the masterpiece to encourage us to look outside the commercially successful and see that art happens all around us.[13] It is not just that art is often intertwined with social and political realities; art that has lost touch with political and social reality is often art that is little more than a capitalist tool.

Some contemporary commercial art has a great deal to offer. Museums, classical concerts, and commercial galleries contain art that opens worlds; in part this is my definition of important art. But powerful art is often found precisely in those locations that are somewhat removed from the institutions of high culture and the circulation of capital. Go to any small or medium-sized city in the United States and you will find music as well as visual art produced by people who cannot support themselves through their art. The great majority of artists are forced to make ends meet by working nonartistic jobs. They paint, sculpt, play musical instruments, and sing without ever being able to devote themselves to this "full time." Melville and Kafka worked their day jobs and then became famous. Most artists labor in perpetual obscurity, known only to a small group of friends; die; and are lost to obscurity. And almost all of us have artistic moments. We take a picture, write a poem or a short story, arrange flowers, sing a song, arrange a room, hang things on a wall in ways that are imbued with rich meanings that can be communicated. When we enter someone's living space, when we observe that person's mode of self-presentation, we are looking into his or her world. These can be important aesthetic moments. Few of us have the technical abilities of Michelangelo or Caravaggio, but many are more artistic than we realize. If we can come to understand art as connected to our social worlds, then we will see how thoroughly vital art can be to exploring who we are. Furthermore, art seen in this way reminds us of its sentinel place in cross-cultural understanding. If we are to understand others, then we must understand something of the nonscientific aspects of their worlds. We will understand each other only if we consider those aspects of our lives that we cannot fully explain but that are vital to who we are. In short, if we want to understand each other across cultural divides, we must look for art that is something more than a mere marketing tool. We must look for art that opens up worlds, and much of this will not be commercially successful.

IMAGE POLITICS

It is difficult to overestimate the amount of politics involved in interpreting art. Who can say what an artwork really means? Is it the property of the community out of which it came? I want to start this discussion by repeating my earlier acknowledgment that white men have often been guilty of misappropriating and misunderstanding the works of others. Chapter 3 discusses hooks's claim that many white critics have failed to appreciate the extent to which Basquiat's art cannot be understood apart from the suffering of African Americans. There are other, in fact, numerous other, examples one could cite of interpreters failing to understand the art of others. At the same time, it is clear that often outsiders can provide important insights into works of art that the insiders have missed. Faulkner was discovered in France before he was widely recognized in the United States. In the case of whites trying to understand the work of African Americans, we must remember not only the long tradition of white exploitation of nonwhite people but also that many whites have traditionally held that blacks are incapable of theoretical reflection. According to white stereotypes, blacks might even be creative geniuses, but whites held the special dispensation of intellectual thought. Given this history, whites who are trying to understand African-American art should begin by acknowledging and then rejecting this legacy of alleged white intellectual supremacy.

I have already spoken of the need to go slowly, exercising caution and humility when trying to understand the art of another culture. But the obstacles should not prevent us from engaging the work of other cultures. One does not have to be from Mississippi to read, admire, teach, and write on Faulkner. One does not have to be an African-American woman to read, admire, teach, and write on Morrison. When faced with art from worlds that are unfamiliar to us, be it art from another continent, or from the other side of the tracks, it is important to talk with those who have more access to the world that produced the art. In those cases where there is a body of critical literature, it is important to read what others have written. It is possible to admire art that one does not really understand. The world is a large place, and our time is limited. Most of us will see art from traditions that we will not have time to research. Our understanding of such art will be limited. Our interpretations of such art will probably say a great deal more about our worlds than about the world out of which that art came. But we should be prepared to talk about and write about those works of art that we do have time to study. Good critical discussions of art help to bring art alive. If, as Adorno and hooks claim, art demands interpretation, then adding our informed voices to the conversation helps to keep art alive.

Not only does the artwork benefit from good critical perspectives from a variety of perspectives, but the interpreter will benefit as well. As any traveler knows, when one leaves the comforts of home one learns not only about others but also about oneself. When we study the art of another culture, we learn of similarities and differences between ourselves and others. We gain critical perspective on our own ways of being. This is particularly true of European Americans who take the time to read the literature of African Americans, Latinos, and Asian Americans. Collins writes of the "outsider-within" perspective of African-American women.[14] Given that many African-American women have worked as domestic helpers inside the homes of white Americans, they have observed white Americans from very close range. We can all learn from seeing how others portray us.

Artists have always had to go beyond themselves in their art. Flaubert created Madame Bovary; Faulkner created a pantheon of African-American characters; Spike Lee has portrayed the inside of a pizza parlor owned and run by Italian Americans, as well as myriad African-American women and a few white women. Very often, European Americans have been accused of creating stereotypical images of African Americans. However, there have also been artists who seem to get it right. One of the first things for white Americans to consider is what Morrison has labeled "the Africanist presence" in the writings of white Americans.[15] Morrison argues that the portrayal of African Americans has been crucial to European Americans' understanding of themselves. In their portrayal of others, in particular in portrayals of African Americans, we see a great deal about how European Americans understand themselves. In particular, for European Americans "Africanism is the vehicle by which the American self knows itself as not enslaved, but free; not repulsive, but desirable; not helpless, but licensed and powerful; not history-less, but historical; not damned, but innocent; not a blind accident of evolution, but a progressive fulfillment of destiny."[16] Try as we may, it is not clear that European Americans will be able to exclude African Americans from their portrayals of themselves. Our self-understanding is intertwined with understanding of others. In listening to the critiques about our portrayals of others we will learn about ourselves and others.

I believe it is possible not only to understand art across cultural borders, but also to create art using material that lies outside our cultural spheres. To conclude, I examine what hooks has written about Spike Lee's portrayal of African-American women as well as the controversy surrounding John Ahearn's portrayal of two African Americans and one Hispanic American that he created for a plaza in the South Bronx and then removed. These two examples will help us see some of the problems that arise when artists move beyond their immediate cultural spheres. These examples also illustrate how the boundaries of cultural realms are not as simple as they sometimes appear. Race, particularly in the United States, is a complex border. The cases of Lee and Ahearn also graphically illustrate how race, class, and gender work together to define who we are and how we view the world.

Spike Lee burst onto the scene with *She's Gotta Have It* and has been at the vanguard of an important group of young filmmakers ever since. He has produced an impressive body of work in a very short time. In my opinion, he is one of the most interesting directors working today, but several African-

American women have critically interrogated his portrayals of black women. Hooks has criticized Lee's portrayal of African-American women as hollow and stereotypical. In particular, she has criticized *She's Gotta Have It* and *Do the Right Thing*. About *Do the Right Thing* hooks wrote: "Spike Lee may think that he is simply putting it out there the way that it is, but he is doing much more. By portraying the subtle and not-so-subtle, sexist humiliation of black females by black men in the ways that depict us as cute, cool, heavy, he reinscribes those paradigms."[17]

But hooks is not saying that Lee cannot or should not attempt to portray African-American women. In a review of Lee's film *Girl 6* that hooks entitles "good girls look the other way," she argues that *Girl 6* "offers the most diverse images of black female identity ever to be seen in a Hollywood film."[18] On the surface, *Girl 6* is the story of an African-American woman trying to make it in Hollywood. Unable to break into films (in part because she refuses to allow her body to be exploited), she turns to a job in phone sex to pay the bills. Hooks writes that *Girl 6* ("Girl 6" is the name this woman receives while working in her phone sex job) is unable to find any visions of liberatory sexuality. She is limited to the roles of victim, vamp, or castrator. Her sexuality is reduced to nothing more than a response to the patriarchal imaginary. She ends the essay by citing Drucilla Cornell's call for the creation of a space where women's sexual voices—in all their diversity—can speak freely. She insists that progressive *men and women* have a role to play in the creation of this space and suggests that through this critique *Girl 6* makes an important contribution.

When hooks criticizes Lee's portrayal of women, she is not demanding that films be politically engaged in any narrow sense, but she does demand that films that merely reproduce prevailing stereotypes be called into question for their lack of critical insight. We have known, at least since Plato, that artists do not have to tell the truth, but artists who merely reproduce stereotypes do not open up worlds. Uncritical use of stereotypes represents a failure to investigate the life world of one's subject. Men have frequently been accused of misrepresenting women; many African-American women have accused Lee of this.[19] No doubt about it, portraying others is tricky business. The criticisms of Lee show us that even those whom we imagine to be close to the world they portray are sometimes accused of getting it wrong. But if hooks is right, Lee has been at times more successful than others at presenting the complexities of the world of African-American women.

Similar issues of who has the right to work with what images are raised by the work of Ahearn. Ahearn is a white artist who has lived and worked for many years in the South Bronx. Jane Kramer, from whose fine book I first learned about the controversy, and who is still my main source of information about Ahearn's work, reports on the poverty in the neighborhood. It is "part of the poorest congressional district in the country. . . . One hundred and twenty thousand people live there, and a hundred and eighteen thousand are either black or Hispanic. . . . One out of every three adults is unemployed; one out of every four women tests HIV positive when she goes to the hospital to have a baby."[20] Ahearn is a sculptor who is commercially successful. His art consists primarily of casts that he makes of people who live in his neighborhood. He has also done murals in his neighborhood that have been well received by the people who live there. Typically he works on the sidewalk in front of his studio in the South Bronx, making casts of people from the neighborhood. He will give one copy to the subject, and the other may end up in a gallery in Soho. Ahearn won a commission to erect three bronze statues in a traffic triangle not far from where he lives and works. His design passed the community review board. He chose to portray Raymond Garcia, a thirty-three-year-old Latino man who has been in and out of jail, and his pit bull; Daleesha, an African-American teenager who is fourteen, with her roller skates; and Corey Mann, a twenty-three-year-old African American, with a large radio and tape player (commonly known as a "boom box"). The statues were met with hostility, and Ahearn voluntarily, and at his own expense, had them taken down five days after he put them up.

The debate surrounding these statues illustrates, among other things, how the definition of a neighborhood varies. Kramer reports that Garcia believes his community—that is, the people who live in the four buildings between 171st and 172nd Streets, where he, Mann, and Ahearn live—does like the sculptures and wanted them to remain. The sculptures were placed in a small traffic triangle a few blocks away. Mann went to the triangle and discussed them with admirers and defended them from critics. One of the critics of the statues was Alcina Salgado. She has taken a major role in cleaning up her neighborhood. Her apartment actually overlooks the small triangle on which the statues were placed. Kramer reports that she "likes to describe herself as 'the woman who cleans up the place.'"[21] She has also worked hard to make her building clean and safe as well as making sure that the garbage is collected and the hydrants and lights are repaired. Mrs. Salgado compared the statues to the street people who smoke crack on rooftops: people who scared her. Apparently her observations have some truth to them. According to Kramer, Garcia set up Ahearn to be robbed by some of Garcia's friends. Salgado worked hard and helped her own four children to go to college, and she would have preferred to see statues of college kids. Some of those who complained wanted to see statues of Martin Luther King Jr. and Malcolm X, believing that they would be more edifying.

There are at least two questions here. First, how did those who were represented feel? It seems that Garcia and Mann did not object to the images. Kramer does not report what Daleesha (Kramer does not give her last name) thinks of her statue. Garcia was particularly grateful to Ahearn for immortalizing his pit bull in bronze. Second, there is the question of the control of space in one's neighborhood. The controversy, in this case, centers in part on the second question. It is in large part a controversy about the placing of art in public spaces. Middle-class and upper-middle-class African Americans and Latinos were upset by the choice of subjects. Ahearn reports that he removed the statues because he wants his art to make people happy. He admits that originally he wanted to create statues that had an edge, had irony and "complications." That aim he now sees as a mistake. He now is more concerned with making people happy. He now sees the casts he makes to please a neighbor as "purer than something with too much of myself in it."[22] But against Ahearn I would point out that his choice to remove the statues did not make Garcia and Mann happy. Ahearn has a variety of neighbors, and no matter what he does he is going to upset one group. Among other things, this controversy highlights the class diversity within the African-American and Latino communities.

I question whether the goal of meaningful art should be to make us happy. As Wendy Steiner points out in *The Scandal of Pleasure,* art often offends.[23] Be it Salman Rushdie's *The Satanic Verses* or Mapplethorpe's sadomasochistic images, art that probes often scandalizes. The cost of giving up on disturbing or scandalous art is that sanitized art may in the process lose its relevance to our lives. Ahearn's choice to live and work in the South Bronx shows his commitment to portraying the world of his subjects. That his portrayals offended others is in some ways a credit to the ability of his art to open up the world, or at least some of the world, of the South Bronx. Here I would side with Heidegger and say that it is more important for art to open up a world than it is for art to make one happy. This is not to say that I necessarily disagree with Ahearn's decision to remove the sculptures. I am conflicted about this. As I have already said, the decision about whether the sculptures should stay in the place where they were is in part a decision about the control of public space. To argue that I value art that opens up a world is not the same as saying that I believe art should be imposed upon unwilling observers. Mrs. Salgado has perhaps good reason for not wanting to see it outside her window, but there should be a place for it somewhere.

The United States has very little tolerance for those who have served time in prisons. It has also recently decided to abandon its long-standing commitment to supply all children with a minimum standard of living. The opposition of many middle-class African Americans to the statues of Garcia, Mann, and Daleesha mirrors the dominant cultures' tendencies in the United States. What would Ahearn have done if he lived in a majority white community and had portrayed figures that were anathema to the middle-class white community? Would Ahearn have then stood up and fought for the right for those figures to remain on their pedestals in a public place? Would he have voluntarily submitted to the demands of whites to remove the statues of Latinos and African Americans? Would he have cared whether the statues produced happiness in the white viewers?

Racial, ethnic, and gender borders are interrelated and complex. As I have already said, white males in particular are well advised to tread lightly when we approach them.[24] There is a long legacy of white males believing that they understand better and more completely than women of all races and nonwhite males. Often white males believe that they understand women and nonwhite males better than they understand themselves. Ahearn's caution is in some ways a refreshing antidote to some artists' extreme egoism. There is no doubt that we need to tread cautiously when we attempt to portray others, particularly when we attempt to portray others who come from cultures that are quite different from our own. I have said that it is important to have conversations with those who are members of the culture whose art one is trying to understand. This example illustrates once again that cultures are not monoliths. It is difficult enough to judge cultures that we have known intimately all our lives. I wonder whether Ahearn's desire to please is not motivated, in part, by his outsider status. Is it not part of the caution and humility that I said should accompany efforts to understand those who live on the other side of cultural borders? The example illustrates, I think, that there should be limits to our humility and caution. Art often offends, and in particular the art that successfully opens up worlds may be very offensive to many. Unlike Lee, Ahearn is not being criticized for stereotyping, but for presenting unheroic figures. Part of the criticism comes from the fact that Ahearn was so successful in invoking the world of his neighborhood that he actually frightened some of the observers.

If understanding the art of others is really possible, then we must be ready to engage in active conversations with others, and these conversations will inevitably lead to disagreements. Not all whites will agree on Faulkner, not all African Americans will agree on Morrison, just as there were disagreements among Latinos and African Americans about Ahearn's statues. When attempting to understand the art of others we have to go slowly, we have to study and, as I have said repeatedly, apprentice ourselves to the art and to the culture out of which the art comes. But we must be prepared to disagree with each other. I would like to have seen Ahearn stand by his statues, even if I am not exactly sure how he should have done this. I can understand why some would be upset at the statues, but the problem here is not that Ahearn misappropriated or denigrated others. Nor did he produce empty stereotypes. Ahearn knows and understands a great deal of the world out of which his images came. The statues were offensive to some precisely because they revealed a great deal about the world of the South Bronx, and this is reason enough for them to be displayed.

I have argued that not only is politics the legitimate stuff of art, but art will almost always be grappling with the social and political realities of its day. Indeed, the choice to make art dealing with the lives of women and African Americans is a political decision, as is the choice to make art about white males. The notion of the masterpiece is often used in the commerce of art. It can divert our attention from art outside the mainstream. There is a great deal of important art that exists outside the venues of high culture. I am suspicious of art that is closely tied to the capitalist marketplace. Art that opens up a world will not necessarily be art that is commercially successful. Our lives are not carefree, and art that engages our lives will provoke both our joys and that which troubles us. Although I have argued that there are no final authorities on either the interpretation or the use of images, we should exercise caution and humility in both areas. If we engage in serious and prolonged discussions about art with others, there will be disagreements. To understand each other does not mean that we will always agree with each other, nor does it mean that we will always agree about the use of images. Our disagreements will often, but not always, be painful, but they will also provide us with opportunities to gain new perspectives on ourselves and others. The art that I care about does not necessarily make me happy, but it does keep pushing me to think about my own world and the worlds of others.

NOTES

1. The *New York Times* (September 10, 2000), 20, reports that according to the United State's Agriculture Department, 31 million people grappled with hunger or the fear of hunger in the United States in 1999. Approximately 12 million of those were children. This means that 17 percent of all children in the world's richest nation either went hungry or lived in fear of going hungry, at a time of unparalleled prosperity.

2. As Preben Mortensen argues, one can see the absurdity of trying to argue, as Jerrold Levinson and Jerome Stolnitz do, that art should be interpreted without reference to social, economic, and political factors. Stolnitz argues that *"Guernica* has nothing whatever to do with Guernica" (quoted in Mortensen, *Art and the Social Order,* 173). Mortensen argues that our notion of art must be seen in its social and historical contexts. See Jerrold Levinson, "Extending Art Historically," *Journal of Aesthetics and Art Criticism* 51 (1993): 411–24; Preben Mortensen, *Art and the Social Order: The Making of the Modern Conception of Art* (Albany: State University of New York Press, 1997); Jerome Stolnitz, "The Actualities of Non-Aesthetic Experience," in *Possibility of the Aesthetic Experience,* ed. M. H. Mtias (Boston: Dordrecht, 1986).

3. Patricia Hill Collins, *Black Feminist Thought: Knowledge, Consciousness, and the Politics of Empowerment* (New York: Routledge, 1991). For her discussion of these controlling images in particular, see chapter 4.

4. Morrison, prior to the publication of *Paradise,* addressed the Anita Hill–Clarence Thomas debate in an essay introducing the anthology she edited devoted to this event. Morrison uses the story of Friday and Robinson Crusoe to argue that Thomas abandoned the African-American community and was therefore left without a voice. Morrison explains that she was publishing this anthology because she believed that "one needs perspective, not attitudes; context, not anecdotes; analyses, not postures," *Race-ing Justice, En-Gendering Power: Essays on Anita Hill, Clarence Thomas, and the Construction of Social Reality,* ed. Toni Morrison (New York: Pantheon, 1992), xi. Hooks addresses the debate in "A Feminist Challenge," in *Black Looks: Race and Representation* (Boston: South End Press, 1992).

5. Pearl Cleage, *Deals with the Devil and Other Reasons to Riot* (New York: Ballantine, 1993). Evidence that this violence against women continues is offered by the Surgeon General's report on sex education, "The Call to Action to Promote Sexual Health and Responsible Sexual Behavior." The report says that "22 percent of all women have been raped, and that 104,000 children are sexually abused each year." *New York Times,* June 29, 2001, A14.

6. Morrison, *Paradise,* 25.

7. Collins, *Black Feminist Thought,* 77.

8. Angela Davis, *Blues Legacies and Black Feminism* (New York: Pantheon, 1998), 117.

9. See Stanley Aronowitz, *Dead Artists Live Theories* (New York: Routledge, 1994), 6.

10. For an excellent critical discussion of Mapplethorpe, see Arthur C. Danto, *Playing with the Edge: The Photographic Achievement of Robert Mapplethorpe* (Berkeley: University of California Press, 1996). For an excellent discussion of some of Serrano's work see the previously mentioned essay by bell hooks, "The Radiance of Red: Blood Works," in *Art of My Mind: Visual Politics* (New York: The New Press, 1995).

11. Max Horkheimer and Theodor Adorno, *Dialectic of the Enlightenment* (New York: Continuum, 1998), 147.

12. Horkheimer and Adorno also discuss this in *Dialectic of the Enlightenment,* 158.

13. For a very good study of how the concept of the masterpiece is tied to commercial interests, see Mary Woodmansee, *The Author, Art, and the Market: Rereading the History of Aesthetics* (New York: Columbia University Press, 1994).

14. Collins, *Black Feminist Thought*, 11–13, 16, 36, 68, 94, 113, 194, 204, 232–33.

15. Toni Morrison, *Playing in the Dark: Whiteness and the Literary Imagination* (Cambridge, Mass.: Harvard University Press, 1992).

16. Ibid., 52.

17. bell hooks, *Yearnings: Race, Gender, and Cultural Politics* (Boston: South End Press, 1990), 182.

18. bell hooks, *Reel to Real: Race, Sex, and Class at the Movies* (New York: Routledge, 1996), 18.

19. See, for example, bell hooks, "Counter Hegemonic Art," in *Yearnings*, 183. See also bell hooks, "Whose Pussy Is This?" in *Reel to Real*, 227–35.

20. Jane Kramer, *Whose Art Is It?* (Durham, N.C.: Duke University Press, 1992), 47.

21. Ibid., 98.

22. Ibid., 111.

23. Wendy Steiner, *The Scandal of Pleasure: Art in an Age of Fundamentalism* (Chicago: University of Chicago Press, 1995).

24. Christine Stansell discusses this issue of the difficulty of whites criticizing African Americans in relation to the Anita Hill–Clarence Thomas debate. She notes that before Anita Hill came forward with her accusations of sexual harassment, Catherine McKinnon, who was known as a "radical feminist," criticized women's groups' opposition to Thomas as too narrow minded. McKinnon spoke of the importance of Thomas's background and believed that it would allow him to understand the reality of everyday people. Stansell argues that, on the one hand, McKinnon's remarks merely show her long-standing flirtation with conservatives that dates from her championing the antipornography movement. "On the other hand they [McKinnon's remarks] show how easily snookered even a sophisticated and militant feminist can be when the issue is racial identity. And on yet another, they embody a long romance of American radicals with some imagined folk authenticity, a form of left-wing condescension that looks for ideas from the privileged and 'life experiences' from the poor." See Christine Stansell, "White Feminists and Black Realities: The Politics of Authenticity," in *Race-ing Justice, En-Gendering Power*, 256.

INDEX

Achebe, Chinua, 122, 127
Adorno, Theodore, 3, 4, 12–13, 99–117, 121, 129, 131; critique of Bach, 119n24; critique of Beckett, 108, 111; critique of Beethoven, 114; critique of Brecht, 110, 115; critique of Dada, 103; critique of Salvadore Dali, 116; critique of Duke Ellington, 113; critique of Hegel, 105–6, 118n9; critique of Kafka, 11; critique of Kant, 103–4; critique of Sartre, 110; *Dialectic of the Enlightenment*, 113, 127–28; interpretation of Eduard Mörike's "Mouse Trap Rhyme," 109; interpretation of Picasso's *Guernica*, 109; mimesis, 105–7; "Pernnial Fashion," 114; rational and irrational theories of art, 102–3; scientific verses artistic understanding, 103; spiritualization of art, 104
Aeschylus, 50
African masks, 6, 7
Ahearn, John, 13–14, 133–37
Apollo, 49–53, 60
Appiah, Kwame Anthony, 16n13
apprenticeship, 8, 11, 74–75, 89–95, 137
Archilochus, 52
Aristotle, 9
Armstrong, Louis, 118n12, 119n22

Aronowitz, Stanley, 138
artwork: definition, 5–7; open up worlds, 11–13, 45, 48, 74–86, 9–95, 100, 122–23, 125, 129–30, 133, 135–37 144n6, 144n13, 146n18; quality of, 6–7, 9, 14n1; understanding, 7–10, 17, 35, 46–47, 53, 74–75, 79, 83–95, 106–17. *See also* social origins of art
Auschwitz, 121

Bach, Johan Sebastian, 36, 121. *See also* Adorno
Bagandan, 75, 91
Baraka, Amiri, 36, 46, 67n3
Basquiat, Jean-Michel, 11,15n11, 73, 83–84, 87–89, 94
Bastille Opera, 128
Beckett, Samuel, 15n11; *See also* Adorno
Berendt, Joachim-Ernst, 101
Bernasconi, Robert, 15n7, 96n15, 97n16
Bernstein, J. M., 38n2
Beethoven. *See* Adorno; Nietzsche
Berlin, 122
blues, 1, 5, 10–11, 45–46, 53, 78, 94; Christianity and, 53
Brecht, Bertolt, 109: *See also* Adorno
Bronx, 133–35
Butler, Judith, 15n3

Caravaggio, 130
Carib, 21, 39n12
Cleage, Pearl, 126
Collins, Patricia Hill, 2, 3, 15n5, 56, 90, 125–27, 131–32
Cooper, Harry, 101
corporate sponsors of art, 5, 123
Crenshaw, Kimberlé, 126
cultural borders, 1–3, 7–9, 14, 17–19, 34, 37, 83, 91, 107, 124, 136
culture industry, 1, 12–13, 115–17, 123, 129, 137, 139n13

Dali, Salvadore. *See* Adorno
Davis, Angela, 1, 2, 3, 11, 46, 53, 56–57, 62–67, 104, 127
de Kooning, William, 87
Derrida, Jacques 3, 12, 40n18, 42n31, 73–89, 95n4, 99–100, 117
Dewey, John, 36
Dionysus, 49–53, 60
Du Bois, W. E. B., 1, 36

East Africa, 6
Ellington, Duke. *See* Adorno
Euripides, 51

Faulkner, William, 15n11, 127, 129, 131, 132
Ferry, Luc, 96n6
film, 5, 121–23, 127
Flaubert, Gustave, 132
Foucault, Michel, 3
Freud, Sigmund, 5
Fynsk, Christopher, 81–83, 96n11

Goldstein, Kurt, 76
Goodman, Nelson, 16n16
Gordon, Louis, 3
Gracyk, Theodore, 118n12, 199n23
Greenberg, Clement, 72n45
Griffith, D. W., 124

Guggenheim Museum: Bilbao, 123
Guyer, Paul, 38n9, 42n32, 43n40

Handel, Friedrich, 36
Hansen, Miriam, 105
Harding, James, 101, 119n22
Hawkins, Coleman, 119n23
Hegel, George. *See* Adorno
Heidegger, Martin, 3, 6, 11–12, 73–89, 94, 96n6, 97n18, 99–100, 107, 122, 135; "Origin of the Work of Art," 73–89; preserving works of art, 83–89, 96n13; Zeug, 77–79, 88, 95n4
Hein, Hilde, 30
Hill, Anita, 125–26
hip-hop, 5
Holiday, Billie, 47, 63–65, 119n23
hooks, bell, 2–4, 6, 9–10, 11, 18, 30–31, 34, 37, 47, 63, 73–89, 94–95, 126, 131; critique of Spike Lee, 132–33
Horton, Willie, 124

Impressionists, 4, 129
interest and interpretation of art, 10, 18, 20–22, 28–32, 37, 39n9, 53
Iroquois, 21

Jay, Martin, 117n5, 118n7
jazz, 12–13, 99–101, 111–17, 119n22

Kafka, Franz, 130: *See also* Adorno
Kant, Immanuel, 3, 10, 18–44, 47, 103; disinterested aesthetic judgments, 20–22; empirical interest for the beautiful, 32–34, 43n41; *Observations on the Feeling of the Beautiful and Sublime*, 18; reflective judgment, 10, 22–28, 41n27; *sensus communis*, 43n39
Kaufmann, Walter, 67n1, 68n11
Keller, Jane, 40–4ln23
Ku Klux Klan, 56

Kramer, Jane, 133
Kristeva, Julia, 3

Lacan, Jacques, 3
Lavater, Johann Casper, 38n5
Lee, Spike, 132–33, 136
Lenson, David, 70n19, 72n44
Levinson, Jerrold, 138n2
life world, 7, 77–81, 123, 182
Lippard, Lucy, 16n14

Makerere University, 75, 91
Makkreel, Rudolf, 25, 40n22, 41n24, 41n27
Mapplethorpe, Robert, 128, 135
Marcuse, Herbert, 48, 63
masterpiece, 5–7, 123–24
McKinnon, Catherine, 139n24
Memphis, 94
Mendelssohn, Moses, 38n5
Michelangelo, 130
Minh-ha, Trinh, 28, 37, 38–39n8
Mitterand, Francois, 128
Mörike, Eduard. See Adorno
Morrison, Toni, 3, 5, 36, 122, 125–27, 129–32, 135, 138n4
Mortensen, Preben, 138n2
Museveni, Yoweri, 91–92

Native Americans, 18
Nietzsche, Friedrich, 3, 10, 42n29, 45–67, 103–4, 114, 125; Bach, 61, 65; Beethoven, 61, 62, 65; *The Birth of Tragedy*, 48–54, 58, 59–61, 68n10, 69n15, 69n16; *The Case of Wagner*, 58, 62, 65, 67n4, 71n31, 72n46, 72n47; decadence, 46; definition of tragedy, 49–53; Goethe, 62; The Good European, 62; Heine, Heinrich, 62; Kant, 60–61, 65; Mozart, Wolfgang, 62; Schopenhauer, 60–61, 65, 70n30; Schuman, Robert, 62; Stendhal, 62; *Twilight of the Idols*, 52, 55, 57–58, 65, 72n51; Wagner, 46, 58–59, 61, 62, 65, 68n12, 71n39, 72n44, 72n47

Paris, 21, 122
Parker, Charlie, 118n12
Picasso, Pablo, 122; *Guernica*, 138n2. See also Adorno
Piper, Adrian, 9, 14n1, 72n45
Pippen, Horace, 13, 36, 112
Plato, 105
Polk, Richard, 67n1
Pollock, Jackson, 13, 87, 112
Pompidou Center, 123

quilts, 5–6, 7

racial divide, 2
Rainey, Gertrude, "Ma," 45, 46, 53, 56, 63
Rauschenberg, Robert, 87
Robinson, J. Bradford, 112–13
Rudinow, Joel, 67n3
Ruprecht, Louis, 70n26
Rushdie, Salman, 135
Rwanda, 121

Sallis, John, 69n14, 69n16, 70n19, 70n23, 70n25, 71n43, 80, 83, 95n2
Sapphire, 116
Sarajevo, 121–22
Sartre, Jean-Paul 7, 89–90, 93, 97n19. See also Adorno
Sartwell, Chrispin, 15–16n15
Sbernicia, 121
Schank, Gerd, 67n2
Schopenhauer, Arthur, 71n33
scientific explanations, 4–5, 14, 89; Heidegger's relationship to, 97n18
Scott, Jacqueline, 58
Seiber, Mátyás, 119n22
Serrano, Andres, 128
Shakespeare, William, 4, 5, 108

Shapiro, Meyers, 12, 73–80, 86–89, 94, 99–100
Simpson, Lorenzo, 3, 115, 116
Simpson, O. J., 2, 125
Smith, Bessie, 1, 45, 46, 53, 56, 63
social origins of art, 11, 57–58, 59–67, 88, 99, 102, 115–16, 122–23, 129, 137
Socrates, 51
Sontag, Susan, 122
Sophocles, 50
Spelman College, 2
Spelman, Elizabeth, 16n12, 89–90, 97n19
Spielberg, Steven, 116
Ssengendo, Pilkington, 75, 91–94
Stansell, Christine, 139n24
Steiner, Wendy, 135
Stolnitz, Jerome, 138

Taylor, Paul, 15n10
Thomas, Clarence, 125–26
Todd, Ceil, 91
Tonelli, Giorgio, 22, 39–40n15, 40n26
Townsend, Peter, 119n24
Twombley, Cy, 87
Tyson, Mike, 125

Uganda, 91–94
understanding artworks. *See* artworks; apprenticeship

Van Gogh, Vincent, 12, 73–89, 94, 112, 129
Vaux le Vicomte, 29–30
Versailles, 29–30

Wagner, Richard, 46
Walker, Alice, 5
Warhol, Andy, 11
Washington, Desire, 125
West, Cornel, 2, 3, 4, 10, 18, 36, 90, 126
Wilke, Sabine, 118n14
Willett, Cynthia, 7n15
Williams, Patricia, 2
Williams, William Carlos, 109
Wilson, Jeffery, 41n23
Woodmansee, Mary, 139n13

Young, Julian, 68n13, 69n17

Zangwill, Nick, 39n9
Zammito, John, 38n5
Zuidervaart, Lambert, 118n11

ABOUT THE AUTHOR

James Winchester is assistant professor of philosophy at Georgia College and State University. He is the author of *Nietzsche's Aesthetic Turn: Reading Nietzsche after Heidegger, Deleuze, and Derrida*. He is currently working on a manuscript exploring ethical responsibilities in the face of today's global inequalities.